BILLY KAY

# Scots
# The Mither Tongue

**GRAFTON BOOKS**

A Division of the Collins Publishing Group

LONDON  GLASGOW
TORONTO  SYDNEY  AUCKLAND

Grafton Books
A Division of the Collins Publishing Group
8 Grafton Street, London W1X 3LA

Published by Grafton Books 1988

First published in Great Britain by
Mainstream Publishing Company (Edinburgh) Ltd 1986

ISBN  0-586-20033-9

Printed and bound in Great Britain by
Collins, Glasgow

Set in Times

Educated at Kilmarnock Academy and Edinburgh University, much of Billy Kay's work has been devoted to creating an awareness of Scottish culture, especially the working-class culture he recorded in his 'Odyssey' series on BBC Radio and TV.

For ma mither, Anne Adams Kay

1922–1984

'. . . till a' the seas gang dry'

# Acknowledgements

I should like to thank the following people for their help, advice and contribution of material for the book:-my editor, Iseabail MacLeod; Eleanor Aitken, Director of 'The Mother Tongue', and Bruce Young, Producer of 'The Scots Tongue', the companion Television and Radio series broadcast by BBC Scotland; my tutor in Scots at Edinburgh University, A.J. Aitken; Carol Craig; J. Derrick McClure; Dr. William Donaldson; Keith Williamson; Alexander Law; Dr. David Hewitt; David Purves; William Neill; R.D. Clement; W.A.D. Riach; Suzanne Romaine; Nancy C. Dorian; P.H. Scott; Hans Speitel; Tom Leonard; William McIlvanney; Gordon Williams; Walter Elliott; Linde Lunney, Jack McKinney, Ernie Scott of Ulster; John J. Graham and the Sandison family, Shetland; Ian D. Hendry; Duncan Muirden; Ellie McDonald; the staff of Edinburgh University Library; the staff of the Scottish Library, Central Library, Edinburgh; Bill Campbell, Peter Mackenzie and the staff of Mainstream Publishing; James Hutcheson; Scottish Arts Council, Literature Department, for a Travel and Research Grant; Alex Watson and Digital Publications; ma wife João an dochter Joanna for their support; ma mither an faither at gied me Scots . . an gart me be prood o it.

# Contents

Chapter 1:     *The Mither Tongue?*                    13

Chapter 2:     *The Beginnings.*                        27

Chapter 3:     *Langage of Scottis Natioun.*            41

Chapter 4:     *Two Diadems in One.*                    59

Chapter 5:     *The Confusion of Union.*                75

Chapter 6:     *The Vernacular Revived?*                93

Chapter 7:     *The Last Scotch Age?*                  111

Chapter 8:     *Renaissance and Erosion.*              125

Chapter 9:     *Wha's Like Us?*                        139

Chapter 10:    *The Dialects of Scots.*                149

Chapter 11:    *The Future Oors.*                      169

Further Reading and Bibliography.                      181

THE DIALECTS OF SCOTS
DRAWN BY CAILEAN MACLEAN
TAKEN FROM THE SCOTTISH NATIONAL DICTIONARY

# Chapter 1

## The Mither Tongue?

The guid Scots tongue. . . a slovenly debased dialect. . . the Doric. . . corrupt English. . . artificial Lallans. . . uncouth gutturals. . . the National Language. . . an unintelligible dialect of English. . . Braid Scots. . . coarse slang. . . a language that never existed – every one of those terms and epithets has been used to describe the language I was brought up to speak, Scots. Its sounds are still the ones which rise most naturally to my lips and therefore haunt the very writing of this book. The ideas often come in Scots, and the previous passage could just as easily be transcribed as: every ane o thae terms an epithets has been uised tae describe the language I wes brocht up tae speak, an its soonds is aye the anes that rise maist natural tae ma lips. Thinking in Scots and writing in English, switching from Scots to English when the social situation calls for a change of register, getting into a muddle or "puttin yer fuit in it" when the switch is not a clean one and Scots invades the English – all are part of the linguistic experience of most Scots raised in the Lowlands – and that covers the great majority of the population. For many, admittedly, the change from one register to another is not as dramatic as in my case, where a very rich dialect of Scots prevails. In the cities English and Scots have come closer together, though less so than many would have us believe. In the country and towns on the other hand speech patterns persist which are little changed in structure from the Scots spoken in the language's Golden Age of the 16th century. When Scots speakers use the full canon of their dialect, not only the sounds and words vary greatly from the English equivalent, but also syntax and grammar: "Afore I gaed ower the brig, the toon nock chappit hauf twa an thir lassies spierit gin I had got lousit shuiner nor I ettled". "Before I went over the bridge the town clock struck half past two and these girls asked if I had stopped work sooner than expected". Even among older people who speak a much more conservative form of Scots than anyone of my generation, the more usual form of communicating that information would be in a mixture of the two registers, with the balance of the mixture depending on the circumstances. In my own case, the mixture in normal circumstances would be close to the following: "Afore I went ower the brig the toon nock chappit hauf twa an thir lassies asked if I had stopped work shuiner than I expected". Now all three versions communicate the information equally well, but the reaction to the three variations would be as diverse as some of the descriptive epithets used at the beginning of this chapter.

Alongside the Scots of my community, I acquired knowledge of English, as it was the medium of education, the Kirk, the doctor's surgery and the radio and eventually television which exerted strong cultural influence on the home environment. English was very much a written medium for me however, and it was only really when I went to university that I felt the need to communicate for any sustained period in standard English. Tongue-tied initially, because I doubted my ability to speak fluently in that register, I eventually sat down with tomes of classic English novels by authors like Thackeray and Austen and attempted to master their dialect. To this day my English resounds with words like propensity and impropriety! Having acquired spoken English and feeling confident in my ability to communicate in it, I also made the conscious decision that knowledge of English did not necessitate the eradication of Scots. One of the most debilitating phenomena of Scottish society is the false notion that to get on you have to get out. English hegemony is so all-pervasive, that a sign of success and sophistication among some is to attempt to erase signs of Scottishness from their public persona. The implications of such an attitude for Scottish culture are drastic, not to mention wrong-headed. The linguistic tension is often not resolved at one particular time of life, and can be an ongoing choice throughout one's life. Some people pretend to lose their Scots at some stage, then magically regain it later on because their social circumstances or cultural allegiances have altered. I recall an incident at Edinburgh University where at a social gathering someone accused me of putting on unnaturally a Scots dialect, because I used the word twa instead of two.

The same gentleman now teaches in a working-class school, and uses twa as "unnaturally" as I used to do. For me, then, not to continue using Scots would have been tantamount to rejecting the culture of the people I came from, and hacking off the cultural roots which gave me the strength of identity I am lucky to possess. Discovering at university that to my great surprise the culture I came from had a literature and a history and its language a pedigree, made me resolved rather to explore and strengthen awareness of the links between the Scottish intellectual tradition and the working-class culture most Scots stem from.

But long before that I had pride in the Scots of my childhood. That was perhaps influenced by the fact that I had the good fortune to be born in the same dialect area as Robert Burns, Kyle in Ayrshire. Along with Elvis in the '50s and the Beatles and Tamla Motown in the '60s his songs were part of the popular working-class culture that surrounded me in Galston and I suppose that helped give our dialect a status perhaps lacking in other airts of Scotland. But when you are young, status is far from your mind – it is just the way everyone spoke to everyone else. It was through the medium of this speech that the world became organised and controlled, and my relationship within it got definition. So much so that I still have to think hard to come up with the English for many everyday words; the birds of the surrounding countryside are still speugs, whaups, peesies, linties, stuckies an mavies to me. My mother, whose childhood had been spent in Mauchline, moved to Bowhill in West Fife with her father, a miner. She brought back to Ayrshire exotic terms such as "baffies" for slippers or "bocht" for unwell and these were absorbed into her family's speech. The family's annual Fair Holiday was spent, or in my father's case, tholed in Bowhill – Galston wi pit bings was an apt description! There everyone spoke Scots as well, albeit with that singsong accent of theirs. As Galston and Bowhill were the limits of my childhood experience, I presumed that everyone in Scotland bar the middle classes spoke Scots. This then was my everyday speech, fundamental to my family, local and national identity and an integral part of my sense of selfhood. Like me, I am sure hundreds of thousands of Scots.

It came as an extreme shock to discover that speaking the everyday language of home in the classroom was regarded as giving cheek to the teacher. The dialect was permitted once a year when the Burns Federation was giving out its certificates or the school was organising a Burns Supper. The rest of the time you would be belted for using his language within the school. Now if one person's being is expressed through a language which is not recognised as a valid means of communication by the authorities which govern his life, the result can be traumatic. I am convinced that thousands of people from the same background as myself have rejected education because they felt its values totally alien from those of their own environment. I was lucky in that languages came easy to me, and I could adapt to the teachers'requirements the few times this was demanded. For others though, the banning of what for some was their only means of communication obviously lead to a taciturn resignation that school was not for them. If using your first language is classed in the same way as sticking your tongue out at the teacher, there is little ground for fruitful dialogue. Educationalists often refer to the Inarticulate Scot, as if it were a hereditary disease, instead of the effect of shackling people with one language, when they are much more articulate in another. The omnipotent standard of having one correct way of speaking colours our society's attitude, and results in false value judgements about people. These value judgements are made in every sector of society, not just in education. When I began the series of interviews of working-class Scots which led to the creation of the Odyssey series on Radio Scotland, a B.B.C. internal report on my progress in the Corporation praised my ability in making inarticulate people talk. In the six months I had been conducting the interviews, I had met nothing but highly articulate characters – the kind of folk that made the series such compelling listening. The report made the typical British error, of judging not what was said, but how it was said – the surface, not the content. The B.B.C.'s policy on language is slowly changing, but they have missed out on a wealth of human experience because of the narrow linguistic range they accepted for broadcast until very recently. The schools too are now more tolerant of local variations of speech, but again they have a lot to answer for with the numbers they alienated with that attitude in the past. And not just in the past. While doing research for this book I was given copies of memos sent to staff by a headmaster of the old guard who subscribed to the myth that Scots is dead and all that remains is slang. The irony is that the school in question is the one Burns would have gone to if he had been alive in Mauchline today. Scots is still strong there, as it is among teenagers in my own home town a few miles away. This was written in March 1985.

> The Doric
> Five of our former pupils have lost their places in offices, under a youth training scheme, because they either could not or would not attempt to speak standard English on the phone. If you allow the use of the doric by your pupils in your room, you could be a contributor to what can only be described as a sorry state of affairs.

The other reference to Scots comes in the rules for teachers printed in 1983. This is no 11.

> *The Doric* is quite often used as a form of insolence. Be on the look out for attempts so to abuse it.

The latter suggests that the headmaster would be happy with a pure and chaste Doric, in which the proprieties are observed, but his teachers assure me that any form of Scots was banned as cheek. In schools now you can have that kind of attitude adhered to in one classroom and the opposite – where articulacy in the dialects is encouraged – operating in the room next door. William McIlvanney recalled for me an incident that occurred when he was a teacher in Kilmarnock. One of his colleagues in the English Department insisted that everyone spoke in standard English. One wee boy found it diffficult to make the switch, constantly referring to haun, fuit, an heid rather than the equivalent English term. Eventually the teacher brought him out to stand in a corner as punishment. He was standing there when the school headmaster walked in and on seeing the boy, said "Oh ho, whit's he been daein noo?" – in exactly the same dialect the boy was being punished for. This kind of anomaly prevails all over Scotland. It is little wonder then, that for some children, fierce loyalty to the dialect and the refusal to adapt to English is a sign of resistance to the rubbishing of their culture that all too many of them experience in school.

My dialect loyalty had elements of that in it as well, but these were in tandem with a positive love for language and all its possibilities. This fascination I am sure arose from the awareness of the different potential one discovered in both childhood registers. The knowledge of Scots also helped in concrete instances. Old John Murray was Provost of the town and a great friend to me as a child. He used to say that the soldiers who came back from the Great War maintained that the Germans could understand them if they spoke broad Scots. When on the first day of learning German the school reader said, Die Tochter milchte die Kuh, I recalled John's words and translated with ease the dochter milkit the coo! French too was tackled with the knowledge that behind le gigot, une assiette, and des groseilles lurked a gigot chop, an ashet for steak pies and the grozets that gave their name to Killie's annual Grozet Fair! Foreign languages with strong links with home. I can think of many other Scots past and present who have the same delight in language which runs counter to the general linguistic chauvinism that prevails south of the Border. Along with the Spaniards, the English have a deserved reputation as the worst linguists in the world. If our attitude to foreign languages is better than theirs, unfortunately we have been infected by the natural corollary of that attitude; that within these islands as without, there is only one "proper" way of speaking and that is Standard English with a Home Counties accent; all other accents, dialects and languages are dismissed as aberrations. Britain is one of the few countries in the world where being monolingual is frequently considered preferable to being bilingual in any of the country's other native languages. Everyone has strong opinions on language because it affects class, social advancement for children, regional and national identity, inferiority and superiority, and ultimately how we see ourselves. Unfortunately, the dearth of Scottish studies in our education system means that many of the strong opinions voiced on the subject are based on half-truths and prejudices rather than actual knowledge of the history of the Scots language.

No doubt the arguments will continue as long as there is a tension between how people naturally speak, and society's attempt to make them speak differently. Of course, that tension exists in English dialect areas too, but what gives the Scots debate its cutting edge is that Scots was once a national language which produced, and continues to inspire a brilliant literary tradition. The dialects of Scots that remain not only express the present, but are also the key to a unique world picture of the past. That is why many people resent, and to some extent resist the steady erosion of Scots. It is also why the arguments will continue, until every aspect of our linguistic inheritance is accorded the same prestige and status as English.

But it is not only the inheritance of dialect speakers in Scotland which comes under threat from this erosion, for Scots and English were different dialects of the same Old English language, and as a result had a huge body of shared expression. This means that many people in Scotland who consider themselves to be speakers of the purest Standard English, use classic Scots, often unwittingly in their everyday speech. To illustrate what I mean, I have concocted an imaginary telephone conversation between two girls, conducted in what most Scots would consider to be perfect English, but which is in fact thrang with expressions and words whose use here is quite different from their use in the English of the sister kingdom, if they are used there at all.

> I was staying with Sharon overnight. Well, yesterday in the forenoon I went to clap her dog . . . I didn't want to let on that I was frightened, but when it barked, I fell and jagged my pinkie on some broken wood – I got a huge skelf and now I've got a really sore hand. That was the most exciting thing that happened, so you didn't miss yourself at all. Here, it's half eleven, I'm away to my bed. See you Monday next, Bye.

The verb "to stay" where the English would use to live, "the forenoon" for the late morning, the verb "to clap" for the English to pat, a "skelf" for a splinter, "to let on", "a sore hand" "you missed yourself" "I jagged my pinkie" "I'm away to my bed" are a few of a thousand expressions native to Scottish English, but foreign to the English of England. Even "half eleven", and the meaning of the "next" in Monday next are peculiar to Scots.

Scots, then, underpins the everyday speech or vernacular of the vast majority of Scottish people, so knowledge of its range of expression, its history, its vast potential for extending our ability to express ourselves, is vital to our own self-awareness. Hugh MacDiarmid, the leading force behind the Renaissance in Scots literature this century, summed up the problem succinctly:

> Tae be yersel and tae mak that worth bein
> Nae harder job tae mortals has been gien.

In Scotland, for long a linguistic battleground based on myths, class bias, and crackpot theories, children find it difficult to be fully themselves, when the language of their home environment is criticised and devalued by a system that is supposed to be educating them to be at one with that environment. That in itself is bad enough, but when much of the speech that is criticised is not "Bad English" but "Good Scots", the historic national tongue of the children and the language in which much of their great literature is written, the situation surely becomes untenable. For many of the shibboleths condemned as slang by the ignorant today would have been used by king, courtiers and poets in the Golden Age of Scots culture at the turn of the 16th century. The grammar of Scots often differs from English. Take for example the past tense of the verb to be, which in Scots is ye wes not you were, giving "when wes ye wont tae be sae sweir" in Lyndsay's *Ane Satyre of the Thrie Estaitis*. A Glasgow wean would still naturally say, "when wes ye gaun hame" and not when were you going home. "I says to him", "I gaed hame", "I haena seen her", "Hou monie gaes there?" "Thir apples wes guid" "them that daes that" are just a few examples of everyday contemporary Scots speech which would give most teachers apoplexy, but which have a pedigree going back hundreds of years. Political and social history then can determine that the same language at different periods of time can be defined as gutter slang, or an aureate tongue.

It is almost a case of "The people do not speak properly, elect a new people!" In recent times, however, alternative enlightened attitudes have begun to appear from within Scottish education itself, and papers and pamphlets have been published which recommend tolerance of non-standard English forms of speech in the classroom. In a Scottish Education Department report from 1952 entitled "English in secondary schools" the approved speech of the schools are listed as "an exemplar of English generally acceptable to educated Scots" and "words and phrases of genuine dialect, whether of the Borders or of Buchan." For most Scottish teachers, however "genuine dialect" is never the local one, and this applies from Buchan to the Borders and includes every city town and village en route. As long as Scots is in the past, in the country, in the literature, anywhere in fact but in the mouths of children that speak it naturally, it is acceptable. But as soon as it has to be confronted locally it tends to be dismissed. After all, it is spoken mainly by the working class – and their speech could never be accepted as a model. In the late '70s and early '80s when interest in Scottish culture was on a high because of the intense political debate surrounding the Devolution referendum, a number of excellent consultative papers were produced. The best of them "Scottish English: the language children bring to school" came to this conclusion:

> In the Scottish primary school teachers will meet children using language that ranges from the rural tones of a farming community to the possibly more abrasive tones of a city street. We cannot regard this language as some kind of personal aberration nor a reflection of the bad speech habits of parents. Regarded at national level the child's language is a continuation, even in an eroded form, of that language through which for centuries people living in Scotland have expressed their awareness of their own individuality and their sense of inhabiting this place, Scotland. At a personal level it is the child's own language through which he carries on the business of living in a community and must be worthy of respect . . . Can Scottish teachers not accept that diversity in language may be a source of strength and not of weakness? Will the pupil who feels secure in school in his own language and in the language of school not have a better opportunity of using the experience he brings to school – and thereby realising his individual potential – than the pupil who may feel he is entering a world where his language, and all the individual and group experience it carries, is not highly regarded? All we have to work with is the language and the embedded experience that a child brings to school. We cannot reject this.

The momentum for a radical change in attitude to Scots did have an effect, but like all things Scottish it has waned in the post–Referendum apathy that has dogged the Scottish cultural scene in the '80s. More Scottish literature is now taught and a good number of teachers, especially in primary schools have implemented such reports' recommendations. But those who do so still feel they are working in a vacuum, "enthusiastic amateurs trying to support a national culture", as one headmaster put it. For none of the Education Authorities has ever stated that Scottish Literature and Language should be an integral part of the curriculum – the native culture is treated as of peripheral interest, to be taught if the teacher is interested and if time permits! Despite the small advances made in the past decade, the myth of Scots as a debased form of English often prevails. As we shall see, the myth has a long and complex pedigree and no doubt will continue for a long time to come.

What I want to stress in this book however is that Scotland is not unique in this, for most of the nation states of Europe have similarly rewritten linguistic history to justify the neglect of the culture of their so-called minority languages. There are millions of people in Europe whose culture is likewise based on the use of two languages. In Spain, for example, the Spanish equivalent of "talk proper" was "habla cristiano" (speak the language of Christians), a policy executed by the Spanish state but resisted with varying degrees of success by eight million Catalans, two million Basques and three million Galicians.

Scots is a similarly disadvantaged language, broken up into dialects which often express a strong regional rather than national identity; in the North-East for example the common term for Scots is the Doric, in Shetland it is da Shetland tongue, and often town dwellers refer to the dialect as e.g. Selkirk or Kilmarnock rather than give it the national term, Scots. Linguists attempt to define it variously as a *halbsprache* or half language, a deposed language, or a national variety of world English. People who believe in the dominance of a single language dismiss it as just another uncouth regional dialect, like say Lancashire or Somerset, desperately trying to think of one internationally-respected writer who has enhanced those dialects. All ways of speech should be valued, but there is no equivalent of Scots anywhere else in the English-speaking world; Scots have an identity with and loyalty to Scots which is unparalleled in any other area. The contrast can be ascertained by simply crossing the river Tweed at Coldstream and Cornhill, where all but the deaf will hear the difference. There is little left of Northumbrian on one side of the Border, but there is a lot left of Scots on the other. Coldstream bairns have all the words of the English children for use in the classroom, but they also have a very different, additional vocabulary for everyday use; lugs and ears, een and eyes, dook and swim, breeks and trousers etc etc. They are the perfect example of the case for Scots, for these children's horizons are extended by having the two registers. Curiously, the scene in the first of the television programmes, 'The Mother Tongue' where this fact was illustrated was the one that provoked the most delight, and the greatest ire. "A set up", "an artificial distinction" were typical reactions from the group which cannot bear to think of Scotland and England having separate cultures in any way. The most outrageous response came from a Lancashire minister resident in Scotland. He decided that the scene arose from "..the horrible chauvinism which caused suffering to my children at one time and some difficulties for myself [and] is not to be encouraged. It is unchristian, irrational and reminds me of certain people in brown shirts.." Having heard most of the arguments before, the only part of that insane outburst that got to me was the reference to Brownshirts on the Border! As the grandson of two Communist miners, it literally made me see red.

Interestingly, the Border is becoming more and more distinct linguistically as the 20th century progresses. Because of the historic pull of London on the English Borderers and Edinburgh on the Scots side, the greatest concentration of distinctive linguistic features in the whole of the English-speaking world is to be found along the length of that Border. The originally shared dialect had long developed separate features because of the different political orientation of both areas, and now these differences are being heightened rather than diminished by the pressures towards standardisation on either side of the Border. Features of the English Northern dialects are being eroded at a far faster rate than those of Scots. This is probably due to the national identities of either side influencing the way they regard the dialects. For the Scots it is one of their distinguishing badges of identity, while for the English the dialect is increasingly and erroneously perceived as Scots – a linguistic identity they want nothing to do with. A Swiss linguist, Beat Glauser, has done exhaustive research into the speech of the area and has published his findings in a fascinating book, *The Scottish–English Linguistic Border*, which surveys the survival of traditional dialect in the area. Here are his findings on some of the old plurals once common to Scots and the dialects of Northern England:

> According to my material, the line between kye, shuin, een and cows, shoes, eyes is now practically identical with the

Border. . . On the English side of the Border, instances of the old plural forms are rare. Some informants do remember them when asked, but most of them would not use them any longer. Only towards the south of Northumberland and Cumberland are there a few informants that make use of kye, shoon or een.

Noting that many of his English informants actually referred to the words as Scottish, he sums up as follows.

The conclusion sounds paradoxical. As far as the old plurals are concerned, Northern England seems to be "englified" in a southern direction, originating from artificial distinctions between Scottish and English as drawn by the population in the Border area.

The actual Border appears to act as a focus for the respective cultural identities of the two nations. The differences are exaggerated there, presumably because of the frontier mentality. Away from the physical Border, the English appear happier with their dialect, possibly because they do not think of it as Scots. This was the phenomenon that those gorgeous weans in Cornhill and Coldstream so vividly and endearingly demonstrated. The point was not to show that two different languages existed, but that the Scots bairns were bilingual to a degree that has disappeared from the English children. The positive feature in this is that they all seem perfectly happy with their lot.

Despite all the pressures, Scots survives. But if it is to resist the threat of erosion posed by the mass media of the 20th century, it must become an accepted part of our schools' curriculum. The fact of such an important part of the common heritage of Scottish children not being taught would be regarded as unthinkable or at the very least strange in any other civilised nation. Yet, so powerful is English cultural ascendancy in the British Isles, that it is the desire to teach them their heritage which is regarded as so strange, that very few even question the matter. Fortunately, most Scots today are happy with their Scottish accents and their Scottish English – so we have progressed from the ludicrous situation of the 18th century, although some are still conditioned to look down on the uniquely Scots element in our speech. Yet to deny part of our heritage, is to deny part of ourselves and the people we stem from. I stem from Ayrshire and Fife miners who spoke nothing but Scots, and they are part of an unbroken line which goes back to the Scots of the Makars. English is also part of that heritage, and should be valued as a means of communicating with the world. But our English linguistic heritage seems able to look after itself; it is the other tongues, Scots and Gaelic, we need to promote. If we don't, we are in danger of becoming strangers to the cultural background that made us what we are. Unlike Gaelic, Scots and English are closely related and are mutually complementary – two branches of the same tree which nevertheless express very different world pictures. We can and should be at home with both. It would be a tragedy if Scots children became like the unfortunate deracinated Gaels of the cities who sing Gaelic songs in a native tongue they don't understand. For if we lose Scots we lose the key to how people have lived, loved, thought and played in our part of the world for many centuries. It leas a gey tuim feelin, the very thocht. It need not and must not happen.

# Chapter 2

## The Beginnings

> Often the Scots writer is quite unaware of this essential
> foreignness in his work; more often, seeking an adequate word
> or phrase, he hears an echo in an alien tongue that would
> adorn his meaning with a richness, a clarity and a conciseness
> impossible in orthodox English. That echo is from Braid Scots,
> from that variation of the Anglo-Saxon speech which was the
> tongue of the great Scots civilisation.
>
> Lewis Grassic Gibbon.

Lewis Grassic Gibbon gives eloquent testimony to the linguistic
duality of most Scots today. He also reminds us of the ancient
pedigree of the Scots language, which is spoken by most of us,
and haunts the rest. Champions of a language, like Gibbon,
often cite its antiquity to strengthen its claim to be recognised as
the true national tongue. Well, neither Scots nor Gaelic speakers
can claim to speak the language of the country's distant past.
When the Gaels arrived in Argyll around the fifth century and
the Angles in what is now the Eastern Border in the seventh
century, what they found both in the Pictish North and the
Cumbric South were tribes speaking a British Celtic language, or
languages, related to modern Welsh. Indeed much early Welsh
heroic poetry is set in the regions of Lothian and Strathclyde.
Welsh place names abound all over Scotland: *aber* a river mouth
gives Aberdour and Aberdeen; *pen* a headland or hill gives
Pencaitland *pen ced llan* the enclosure in the wood on the hill.

While Pictish symbol stones give insight into the art of the
Picts, not a line of their language comes down to us today.
However in eastern Scotland, north of the Forth, there are
over 300 place names with the prefix pit, from *pett* a share
or portion of land; Pitlochry in Perthshire is the stony share,
Pitcaple in Aberdeenshire is the horse share, and Pittencrieff
in Fife is the share of the tree. They are almost certainly of
Pictish origin and although most of the second elements of these

*pit* names are Gaelic, they provide one of the few indications of the extent of Pictish lands in Scotland.

Another piece in the linguistic jigsaw that became Scotland is provided by the Norsemen whose Scandinavian tongue survives in place names as far apart as Shetland, the Western Isles, and Dumfriesshire. The Norse colonization of the Northern Isles around the year 800, and their subsequent expansion into Caithness and the Hebrides gives us, for example, names coined from the Norse word for a farm *bolstathr*; Norbister in Shetland, Scrabster in Caithness, and Leurbost in Lewis. The Scandinavian influence in the South-West of Scotland came later with settlers from the North-West of England who had a mixed English/Norse background, and another group of settlers from Ireland with a mixed Gaelic/Norse background. Lockerbie and Denby from the Old Norse *byr* a farm are examples of the former's influence, while Kirkbride and Kirkcudbright from Old Norse *kirkja* a church, are examples of the latter.

Thus in tenth-century Scotland five languages were spoken, the Gaelic of the West Highlands, the Pictish of the North-East, the Norse of the Isles, the Welsh of the central and western Lowlands and the Inglis of the South-East. This Inglis later became known as Scots, and is the ancestor of both the dialects of Scots and the Scottish English spoken by all Scots today. Norse, Pictish and Welsh have of course disappeared over the centuries and there are no adult monolingual Gaels left in Scotland today, though thankfully around 80,000 people speak both Gaelic and English. But for Gaelic to survive, it will have to go against the current of language history in Scotland and indeed Britain, for periods of bilingualism have always been followed by the eventual eradication of the less powerful language. This has always been bound up with politics and the prestige that politics confers. It is the same today as it was when Gaelic was devouring Pictish, Norse and Welsh in its aggressive expansion out of its original western settlement.

The impetus behind the rise of Gaelic was provided by both military might and political power, which gave the language social status. Kenneth MacAlpin crushed Pictish resistance in the mid ninth century and absorbed the Picts into his kingdom of Alba or Scotland. In the course of the tenth and eleventh centuries Gaelic continued to spread into Welsh Strathclyde and English Lothian as the power of the different ethnic groups ebbed and flowed in Southern Scotland and Northern England. In 1006, Malcolm II, King of Scots united with Owein of Strathclyde to defeat the Earl of Northumbria at Carham, and confirm the cession of Lothian to his authority. When Owein died, Malcolm placed his own grandson Duncan on the throne of Strathclyde. Duncan in turn became King of Scots, and ruled over a land whose borders have changed little since that period. By the eleventh century, then, Gaelic was the language of court and state, of scholarship, of literature and the church. Examples of Gaelic place names exist in almost every corner of the country: *baile* a hamlet gives Balmuir in West Lothian, and Balgownie in Aberdeenshire; *achadh* a field gives Auchinleck in Ayrshire, and Achinraid in Ross-shire; *cill* a cell or church gives Kilbucho in Peebles-shire, and Kilbrandon on Mull.

The language of the Angles, Inglis, brought north from Northumbria into Berwickshire in the seventh century remained the language of a minority in Scotland, but even when the power of Gaelic was at its height and absorbing other linguistic groups, the people of this south-east corner continued speaking Inglis. The area where Inglis was spoken did expand a little in the following centuries, spreading out into East Lothian, the Solway and an enclave in Kyle in Ayrshire; Whittinghame in East Lothian, tells us the name of one of the early Anglian leader – Hwitingaham – the settlement of Hwita's people; *tun* an enclosure gives Haddington in Midlothian; *wic* a minor settlement gives Hawick in Roxburghshire and Fenwick in Ayrshire.

Part of the great northern dialect area of Old English, the Inglis of the settlers was a Germanic language brought to Britain during the folk migrations from Northern Germany by Anglo-Saxon tribes around the fifth century A.D. The earliest example of their language in Scotland is to be found on the beautifully wrought runic inscriptions on the Cross in the Kirk of Ruthwell in Dumfriesshire. They depict passages from a poem called 'The Dream of the Rood' written in the Old English of the seventh century.

> ongeredae hinae god almehtig
> tha he walde on galgu gistiga
> modig fore alle menn
> ahof ic ricnae kyninge
> haelda ic ni dorstae

girded him then God Almichty
gin he stepped on the gallows
for aw mankind-strang willed
wiout fear. I held the Heich
Keing, Lord o Heiven
Bou me doun, I daurna.

If the language of 'The Dream of the Rood' appears distant to modern Scots, it is even more removed from Standard English. Many of the distinctive sounds which characterise Scots and English speech today go back to differences in the dialects of Old English in the sixth century. They may be even older still, as the dialect differences may have arisen before the various tribes left the continent for Britain. The major dialects of Old English, Kentish, West Saxon, Mercian and Northumbrian, probably reflect the pattern of settlement by Angle, Saxon and Jute and their respective dialects in different parts of Britain. Scots is descended from Northumbrian, while Standard English emerged from the East Midland dialect of Mercia. Although markedly different, the Old English dialects did share a common store of vocabulary. Due to the different linguistic developments in the separate states of Scotland and England however, the language of England lost many old words which are retained in Scots. Examples of these include *dicht* to wipe, *sweir* reluctant, *blate* frightened, *reik* smoke, and *greet* to weep. Characteristic Scots sounds too such as *coo* or *hoose* for cow or house, or *richt* and *nicht* for right and night were common to all the Old English dialects, but disappeared from Standard English due to sound shifts which occurred in Southern and Midland dialects. If antiquity is any justification for a language's survival, a special case could certainly be made for Scots against Standard English, as guardian of an older form of English.

This Northumbrian Inglis held on to its heartland in the South-East, while Gaelic made spectacular gains elsewhere in the kingdom until its expansion was arrested at the end of the eleventh century. It was as if Inglis was biding its time until the political moment was right for its star to rise at the expense of Gaelic. The Gaelic Kings of Scotland had already turned their back on their western homelands as Scone, not Iona became their country's spititual centre. Their choice of capitals – Dunfermline, Stirling and Edinburgh – confirms that the political and cultural balance of the country was moving from the west and north to the south and east, in other words from Gaeldom to the Inglis Lothians. There the Scottish court was wide open to influences from the south, and political turmoil in England at the end of the eleventh century was to have far-reaching effects on Scotland's subsequent linguistic history. Here we can pinpoint the exact moment when Gaelic declined as the language of status in Scotland, to be superseded over the following centuries by the Germanic language called variously Inglis, Scots or English.

Malcolm III or Canmore acceded to the throne in 1058. A Gaelic-speaker, he had however spent a good deal of his life at the English court of Edward the Confessor. When the Normans overran England in 1066, the English royal family fled to Scotland, and the Princess Margaret later married the widower Malcolm. The couple's sons Edgar, Alexander and David were profoundly influenced by their years spent at an English court "in the full flush of Normanization". Norman culture enjoyed tremendous prestige all over Europe at this time and was instrumental in reorganising ideas of government, laws and literature from Sicily to Scandinavia. To encourage this civilising influence, David I (1124-53) and his successors granted lands in Scotland to Norman noble families who held lands mainly in the north of England; Bruce, Balliol, Grant and Fraser, to name but a few.

These grantees originally spoke Norman French, but the mass of the people of lesser rank who accompanied them spoke the Northern dialect of English. The same people populated the burghs that were established as centres of royal power all over the Lowland area, from Elgin and Forres in the north to Dumfries and Ayr in the south.

The polyglot nature of the early Scottish kingdom is confirmed in the royal charters of the period which are addressed to the king's citizens – Francis et Anglis, Scotis et Flemmingis or French, English, Scots and Flemish. For the incoming settlers, the burghs were a cross between pioneer outposts and new towns, a melting pot in which Inglis became the established lingua franca. The power of the burghs meant that the local population, Gaelic-speaking on the whole, had to learn Inglis to participate in the trade the towns generated. The economic benefits to the settlers were considerable, with inducements such as two years tax-free allowance to build houses, and a virtual monopoly for the burgesses in the essentials of local and international commerce. The strict control of the burghs is seen in the Burghs Laws passed by David I. Originally in Latin, they were later translated into Scots. Number 81 refers to the burgh watchman, and reminds us of the pioneering fears of settlers surrounded by a potentially hostile hinterland.

> it is for to wyt of ilke house wythin the burgh in the quhilk thar wonnys ony that in the tym of wakying aw of resoun to cum furth, thar sal ane wachman be holdyn to cum furth quhen that the wakstaff gais fra dure to dure, quha sall be of eylde and sal gang til his wache wyth tua wapnys at the rynging of the courfeu, and sua gate sal wache wysly and besily til the dawying of the daye. And gif ony hereof failye, he sal pay 1111d, outtane wedous.

> (*wonnys* dwells; *of eylde* of age; *sua gate* in this way; *outtane wedous* widowers excepted)

Even more English prestige came with the founding of the great monasteries and the arrival of monks from the North of England. By the 14th century, Inglis had become the principal spoken language of all of Lowland Scotland, with the exception of Galloway where Gaelic survived until the turn of the 18th century.

This Inglis which the settlers brought with them was quite different from the Inglis already long established in the Borders. It could be more accurately called Anglo-Danish, for in the Danelaw north of the Humber the Scandinavian tongue held sway from the ninth century and the local variety of English adapted to the language of those in power. Many of the features which distinguish modern Scots from Standard English, came as a result of this Danish legacy: *kirk, kist* and *breeks* for church, chest and breeches; *brig* and *rig* for bridge and ridge; *lowp* for leap, *ain* for own, *strae* for straw, *skirl* for shrill, *mask* for mash. Many of these Scandinavian words are still in everyday use in Scotland, having died out of the English dialects which originally absorbed them – words such as *flit* to move house, *graith* tools or equipment, *frae* from, *lug,* ear, *nieve* fist and *hoast* cough.

Up till now I have been looking at the shared inheritance of Scots and the Northern English dialects. But in Scotland this northern Inglis gradually evolved into the sophisticated language of state of the Stewart Kingdom, and it developed separately from it's sister tongue across an increasingly hostile border. The vocabulary of Scots was enriched by words borrowed from many different sources.

From the twelfth century onwards the eastern ports of Scotland traded extensively with the Low Countries, where they established colonies in Bruges, Middleburg, and Veere. In turn the Scots encouraged Flemish craftsmen, particularly wabsters or weavers, to settle in the expanding burghs. Thus we have the surnames Fleming, Bremner and Wyper to describe the immigrants from Flanders, Brabant and Ypres respectively. They influenced the language as well; *pinkie, golf, scone, howff* are in everyday use all over the country, while others survive in certain dialects; *bucht* sheep pen, *cuit* ankle, *craig* neck, *pleiter* mess, *redd* tidy up, *loun* boy, *hunkers* haunches, and *doited* daft.

The other great trading partner and military ally of the Scots was France, and the language was influenced both by the Norman French of the twelfth-century settlers and by the Central French of the Auld Alliance, the series of treaties which joined Scotland and France in diplomatic and commercial co-operation from the late 13th to the mid 16th century. The administration of the burghs, strongly influenced by the Normans, was carried out by the provost (*prévôt*), and baillie (*bailli*). Anyone walking in the old part of Edinburgh will recognise the French influence on the streets leading off the Grassmarket – the West Port (*porte* gate) and The Vennel (*vennelle* lane). French culture also had a profound effect on English culture, and so both north and south of the Border many French words were in common use. However, while we in Scotland still use many of these words, they have become obsolete in England; *gigot* leg of lamb, *asket* serving dish, *douce* soft or sweet, and *mavis* a thrush. Other borrowings were confined to Scots, mainly at the time of the Auld Alliance: of the scores of possible examples, *fash* to bother, *affeir* to pertain to and *disjune* breakfast, will suffice to give a flavour of the French influence on Scots life.

Nearer home, the Gaelic language added another distinctive element to the vocabulary of Older Scots. Many words refer to major topographical features of the landscape; *glen, ben, loch,* and *strath*. Others are more general; *ingle* hearth, *cranreuch* frost, *tocher* dowry, *sonsie* comely, hearty. The reason why Gaelic did not influence the Lowland tongue to a greater extent lies in the low prestige of Gaelic culture in the rest of Scotland from the Middle Ages. Most Lowlanders had Celtic blood in them, but as they developed a settled agriculture, and established both foreign trade and a town-based way of life, they began to regard the Gaelic way of life with its warfare and cattle raiding as barbaric and despicable. Their attitude has many expressions in Scots verse. Typical is a poem from the late 16th century by Alexander Montgomerie, in which the poet imagines God creating the first Highlander:

> Quod god to the helandman quhair wilt thou now
> I will down in the lawland lord, and thair steill a cow . . . .
>
> ffy quod sanct peter thow will nevir do weill
> and thow bot new maid sa sone gais to steill
> Umff quod the helandman & swere be yon kirk
> Sa lang as I may geir gett to steill, will I nevir wirk.

(*geir* possessions)

Another source from which Scots derived its increasingly distinctive vocabulary, was the language of learning all over Europe in the Middle Ages – Latin. Many of the borrowings are still used in Scots law today: *dispone* to convey land, *homologate* to ratify, *sederunt* meeting, e.g. of the Court of Session. As we shall see, the Scots poets, or makars, also used Latin to affect a highly ornate, "aureate" style in their work, using "sugurit termis eloquent" such as *preclair, matutine, celicall, palestrall, celsitude, pulchritude, supern, lucern* and many other exquisitely mellifluous words. Of a more down-to-earth nature were later borrowings which nevertheless show the continued influence of Latin on Scots right through to the 19th century; every product of the Scottish education system knows those three pillars of wisdom the dominie, the dux and the jannie!!

Before the end of the 14th century Latin and French were the languages of both scholarship and private correspondence among the few who could write. The Anglo-Norman aristocracy spoke Scots by this time, but the prestige of French was such that it continued as the medium of written communication. In England, where the Norman influence on language was more profound, French was to continue as the language of the law until the 17th century. From about 1380 onwards in Scotland, documents and letters begin to appear which are written in the vernacular of the country. A good example of the Scots of the period comes in a letter from James Douglas, Warden of the Marches to King Henry IV of England, dated 26 July 1405. It also gives vivid insight into the cross-border skirmishing and raiding that went on by both sides during what were supposed to be periods of truce. This part of the letter concerns the burning of Berwick by the Scots. It is occupied by the English at the time, but of course the Scots claim it as part of their own sovereign territory.

> Anente the qwhilkis Hee and Excellent Prynce, qwhor yhe say yhu mervalys gretly that my men be my will and assent has brennede the town of Berwik, the qwhilk is wythin Scotlande, and other place in Inglande, in brekyng fully of the sayde trewis; I understand that giff yhour hee excellent war clerly enfourmyte of the brennyng, slachtyr and takyng of prisoners and Scottis schippis, that is done be yhour men to Scottys men within the saide trewis in divers places of Scotlande, befor the brynning of Berwike; the qwilk skathis our lege lorde the kyng and his lieges has paciently tholyt in the kepyng of the saide trewis, and chargit me til ask, and gar be askyte be me deputs redress tharof; the qwhilk my deputs has askyt at dayis of marche, and nane has gotyne; methink of resoune, yhe sulde erar put blame and punitioun to the doarys of the saide trespas, done agayn the trewis in swilke maner, and callys thaim rather brekars of the trew than me that has tholyt sa mikylle injur so lang and nane amends gottyn.

(*skaith* harm, injury; *tholyt* endured, suffered)

By 1424, the stature of Scots was confirmed when it replaced Latin as the official language recording the statutes of the Scottish Parliament. From then on Scots was the official language of state, dealing with the requirements of all national and local legislation, administration and records. An Act of Parliament of James II of 1457 gives an example of the style of the records. It also reveals that our national sporting obsessions have changed little in the intervening years, though thankfully we can enjoy them free of the guilty consciences of our forebears, who really should have been preparing for the defence of the realm.

> Item, it is decretyt and ordanit that wapinschawingis be haldin be the lordis and baronis spirituale and temporale four tymis in the yere. And at the fut ball ande the golf be utterly cryit doun and nocht usit.

(*wapinschawingis* muster of arms)

Scots was also by now the medium of an emerging literature. The oldest fragment of poetry which survives dates from the year 1286, but the version which comes down to us is Andrew of Wyntoun's transcription from his *Orygynale Cronykil of Scotland* of 1424. The verse mourns the death of Alexander III and the period of rare plenty which had blessed his reign. It is also prophetic in an uncannily fey manner which seems to predict the approaching chaos of the Wars of Independence, caused by Alexander's death and his inability to produce an heir for the throne:

> Quhen Alexander our kynge was dede,
> That Scotlande lede in lauche and le,
> Away was sons of alle and brede,
> Off wyne and wax, of gamyn and gle
> Our golde was changit into lede.
>     Crist, borne in virgynyte,
> Succoure Scotlande, and ramede,
> That is stade in perplexite.

(*lauch and le* law and peace; *sons* abundance; *gamyn* mirth; *ramede* remedy; *stade* fixed)

The earliest masterpiece written in Scots actually concerns itself with the events that unknown poet seems to foretell. It is John Barbour's epic poem *The Brus*, which chronicles Robert the Bruce's campaigns during the period of the Wars of Independence. Addressing his troops before the decisive battle of Bannockburn, Bruce exhorts the men, though terribly outnumbered, to fight with the moral force that lies with them. Just in case that isn't enough, he reminds them of the plunder they'll enjoy from the wealthy English, should the day go with them. He lists the factors on the Scots side:

> The first is, that we haif the richt;
> And for the richt ilk man suld ficht.
> The tothir is, thai are cummyn heir,
> For lypning in thair gret power,

To seik us in our awne land,
And has broucht heir, richt till our hand,
Richness in-to so gret plentee,
That the pouerest of yow sall be
Baith rych and mychty thar-with-all,
Gif that we wyn, as weill may fall.
The thrid is, that we for our lyvis
And for our childer and our wifis,
And for the fredome of our land,
Ar strenyeit in battale for to stand
And thai for thair mycht anerly . . . .

(*lypning* counting on)

*The Brus* also contains the famous lines on freedom. What they assert is that the tyranny of the English occupation has bound personal and national freedom inextricably together.

A, fredome is a noble thing,
Fredome mays man to haiff liking,
Fredome all solace to man giffis;
He levys at es that frely levys.

Considering the diverse ethnic and linguistic mixture that existed in Scotland, her sense of nationhood at this early stage of the development of the idea of a shared national identity, is quite astonishing, not to say precocious. Some of Europe's major nation states today such as Italy and Germany would wait another 500 years before their people identified with the country rather than the locality. Edward I of England, Malleus Scotorum, or Hammer of the Scots, by dint of his constant aggression appears not to have hammered the Scots into submission as was his intent; instead like hammer on steel he forged disparate groups of people into a nation.

The Declaration of Arbroath of 1320 offers not only a brilliant case for Scottish independence and demands recognition of that fact from the papacy, it is also the culmination of the struggle by Bruce, Wallace, and most importantly the community of Scotland. The nobility of the Medieval Latin rhetoric loses a little in translation, but the statement is unequivocal.

. . . . for, as long as but a hundred of us remain alive, never will we on any conditions be brought under English rule. It is in truth not for glory, nor riches, nor honours that we are fighting, but for freedom – for that alone which no honest man gives up but with life itself.

That Scots enjoyed being reminded of their heroic past is proven by the success of the other great national epic, *The Actes and Deidis of the Illustre and Vallyeant Campioun Schir William Wallace,* by Blin Hary. Written around 1470 it helped create the legend of Wallace which was still remarkably potent in Burns' day. Writing to John Moore about the major cultural influences on his life and work, he recalls Blin Hary's poem: "the story of Wallace poured a Scottish prejudice in my veins which will boil along there till the flood-gates of life shut in eternal rest". The Wallace is an action-packed tale full of direct and gory confrontation where the English baddies inevitably get what's coming to them. Hundreds of them share the fate of Sir John Butler, who is about to light down on Wallace from his charger, sword in hand:

> Till him he stert the courser wondyr wicht,
> Drew out a suerd, so maid hym for to lycht.
> Abowne the kne gud Wallas has him tayne,
> Throw the and brawn in sondyr straik the bayne.
> Derffly to dede the knycht fell on land.
> Wallace the hors sone sesyt in his hand,
> Ane awkwart straik syne tuk him in that sted.
> His crag in twa, thus was the Butler dede.

> (*courser* charger; *wicht* brave; *the and brawn* thigh and calf; *derffly* violently; *crag* neck)

Wallace then escapes on the horse, determined to avenge the men he had lost in a previous skirmish. His uncle, Sir John Stewart, wants Wallace to resign himself to the hopelessness of further resistance, accept Edward's offer of peace, and reap the benefits of siding with the English. Wallace's reply echoes both the Arbroath Declaration and *The Brus.*

> "Uncle," he said "off sic wordis no mair.
> This is no thing bot eking of my cair.
> I lik better to se the Sothren de
> Than gold or land that thai can giff to me.
> Traistis rycht weill, of war I will nocht ces
> Quhill tyme that I bryng Scotland in-to pes,
> Or de thairfor, in playne to understand."

> (*eking of* adding to)

Now although Scottish patriotism flowed through the vernacular literature, Scots linguistic nationalism did not exist until the end of the 15th century, just after the time that the Wallace was written. Up till then the language of state had been called Inglis, or in its modern form, English, in recognition of its origin and long-established history in Scotland. In the 14th century in fact there was very little to distinguish the Inglis spoken north and south of the Border right down to the Humber. By the end of the 15th century however the Inglis of Scotland had developed most of the features which still characterise the Scots dialects today and distinguish them from the English of the south. Most of the separate borrowings I mentioned earlier had taken place, and the language was approaching a national standard form based on the speech of Lothian and the capital. In England the emerging standard language came from the East Midland dialect and later on the speech of London. Given the linguistic changes, and perhaps more importantly, the continued hostility between Scotland and England, it is hardly surprising that the Scots began giving their national term Scottis, to their language, to separate it from the language of the Inglis or Southren, as they were also called. The terms Inglis and Scottis existed side by side for a time, but Scottis eventually persisted and is still the name we give our language today. The Spanish Ambassador to the Court of James IV, Pedro de Ayala, gave insight into the differences between Stewart Scots and Tudor English when he compared them to Castilian and Aragonese – the dialects which became Spanish and Catalan respectively. It was an apt comparison and a prophetic one, for Catalan and Scots have shared many parallels throughout history. Both languages have had to define themselves against powerful neighbours whose languages gained ascendency in the Spanish and British nation states which attempted to absorb their cultures. But for Scots that would be well in the future, and in the late 15th and early 16th centuries the "langage of Scottis natioun" as Gavin Douglas called it, emerged triumphantly not only as the language of the nation, but as the medium of possibly the greatest literature that existed in the Europe of that day.

# Chapter 3

## Langage of Scottis Natioun

The hundred years preceding the Reformation was undoubtedly the Golden Age of Scottish literature. It is no accident that the flowering of the country's literature coincided with the period that marked the highest point in the developement of the national language. Since that period, geniuses such as Burns in the 18th century, or MacDiarmid in the 20th century have engaged in superhuman efforts to revive the native muse and prove that Scots could still be the medium of great literature. For both of them however it was necessary to go against the trends of their times to write in Scots and certainly in MacDiarmid's case, much of his creative energy was expended in propoganda for the Scots language cause. He had to explain to an increasingly anglicised Scotland what he meant by the rallying cry for his Literary Renaissance, "Not Burns, back to Dunbar". In that cri de coeur, MacDiarmid was holding up for scrutiny a period in which Scottish literature was unselfconsciously national and international, drawing from and adding to the European civilisation of the Renaissance. For the great makars or poets of what we now call Middle Scots, there was no exhausting debate about the status of their language; their creative energy was spent adorning and extending it into the vibrant, flexible, forceful medium which makes their poetry a joy to read today. Concern about the use and prestige of Scots was not common in medieval Lowland Scotland, as it was quite unnecessary; from the King down, everyone spoke, read or wrote Scots and its supremacy was taken for granted. The makars were fostered and nourished by a tradition which valued their contribution to the national life. There is only room for a flavour of their work here, with examples from four of the greatest of them, Henryson, Dunbar, Douglas and Lyndsay.

The greatest achievement of both Robert Henryson (1425-1505?) and Gavin Douglas (1475-1522?) lay in their translation or reworking of tales and poetry from classical sources in the Scottish vernacular. Taking a classical theme and improving the telling of it was one of the ideals of medieval writers, and in doing that they wrought finely-honed poetry which stood entirely on its own merits. Thus when Henryson approached the tale of Troilus and Cressida or Douglas Virgil's *Aeneid*, their aim was not simply direct translation from classical sources, but rather a vigorous creative recreation of the spirit of their work in a recognisably Scottish environment.

The God Saturn in Henryson's *The Testament of Cresseide* appears to have been transported from the Plains of Troy to the Howe of Fife, an the founeran cauld is getting to him.

> His face fronsit, his lyre was lyke the leid,
> His teith chatterit and cheverit with the chin,
> His ene drowpit, how sonkin in his heid,
> Out of his nois the meldrop fast can rin,
> With lippis bla and cheikis leine and thin
> The ice-schoklis that fra his hair doun hang
> Was wonder greit and as ane speir als lang.

(*fronsit* wrinkled; *lyre* complexion; *cheverit* shivered; *how* hollow; *meldrop* mucus; *bla* livid; *ice-schoklis* icicles)

Similarly, when Gavin Douglas transports us to observe the multitude attempting to get the favour of Charon to transport them over the Styx, the ambience is tangibly Northern.

> Thir ryveris and thir watyris kepit war
> By ane Charon, a grisly ferryar,
> Terribil of schap and sluggart of array,
> Apon his chyn feil cannos harys gray,
> Lyart feltrit tatis; with burnand eyn red,
> Lyk twa fyre blesys fixit in his hed;
> Hys smottrit habyt, owr his schulderis lydder,
> Hang pevagely knyt with a knot togiddir.
> Hym self the cobill dyd with hys bolm furth schow,
> And, quhen hym list, halit up salys fow.
> This ald hasart careis owr fludis hoyt
> Spretis and figuris in hys irne hewit boyt,
> Allthocht he eildit was or step in age,
> Als fery and als swippir als a page;
> For in a god the age is fresch and greyn,
> Infatigabill and immortal as they meyn.
> Thidder to the brae swarmyt all the rowt

Of ded gostis, and stud the bank about,
Baith matronys and thar husbandis all yferis,
Ryal princis, and nobill chevaleris,
Smal childering and yong damysellis onwed
And fair springaldis laitly ded in bed . . . . .

(*feil* many; *cannos* hoary; *lyart feltrit tatis* withered matted
tufts; *smottrit* stained; *lydder* slouching; *pevagely* squalidly;
*cobill* small boat; *bolm* pole; *hasart* grey haired man; *eildit was*
was grown old; *fery* nimble; *swipper* quick; *yferis* in company;
*springaldis* youths)

While using classical sources, the makars employed verse forms
and poetic devices which were rooted in the native tradition,
and complemented the native language. Henryson's versions of
Aesop's fables for example are full of alliterative lines which
strengthen the poet's descriptive power. In 'The Taill of the
Foxe that begylit the Wolf in the schadow of the Mone', for
example, there is a brilliant depiction of a sleekit fox slipping
out of his dark hiding place, "Lowrence come lourand – for
he lufit nevir licht . . ." William Dunbar (1460?-1520?) was
the most technically accomplished of the medieval makars,
absorbing English, French and Latin influences, yet expressing
them in a vigorously Scottish form. He too is a master of the old
alliterative style which he makes great use of in his bawdy poem
of female sexuality, the 'Tretis of the Tua Mariit Wemen and
the Wedo'. This is one of his fair damsels describing her husband:

To see him skart his awin skyn grit scunner I think.
When kisses me that carybald, than kyndyllis all my sorrow
As birs of ane brym bair, his berd is als stiff,
Bot soft and soupill as the silk is his sary lume.

(*scart* scratch; *scunner* revulsion; *carybald* cannibal; *birs* hairs;
*brym* fierce; *bair* boar; *sary lume* sorry tool)

But if his Scots was capable of gutsy colloquial invective, it
was also capable of transforming itself into a highly polished
"aureate" tongue which sought to compete with the prestigious
Latin poetry and rhetoric in elegance of style. In 'Ane Ballat
of Our Lady', Latin mells with Scots with dazzling effect:

Empryce of prys, imperatrice,
  Brycht polist precious stane,

Victrice of vyce, hie genitrice
  Of Jhesu, lord soverayne:
Our wys pavys fra enemys
  Agane the feyndis trayne,
Oratrice, mediatrice, salvatrice,
  To God gret suffragane:
  Ave Maria, gracia plena,
  Haile sterne meridiane,
Spyce, flour delyce of paradys
  That baire the gloryus grayne.

(*pavys* shields; *feyndis trayne* feinds' followers; *grayne* seed)

That poem shows Dunbar as a virtuoso showing off the glittering artefact he can fashion with words. In an exaggerated form both poems reveal the range that was available to speakers of Scots in those days: the higher register of the educated few, replete with foreign words and adaptations; the everyday language of the majority very close to its Anglo-Saxon origins. This social differentiation in registers of Scots is exploited by Sir David Lyndsay (1490?-1555) in his play *Ane Satyre of the Thrie Estaitis*. Criticism of the corruption in the church runs through the play, and it can be read as a forewarning of the inevitability of the coming Reformation. Satire against the priests' vices of sexual excess and exploitation of the poor exist in the speeches by both Sensuality and John the Commonweal, but the registers of Scots they employ are quite different. This is Sensuality's address to her Goddess, Venus.

O Venus goddess, unto thy celsitude
I give laud, gloir, honour and reverence,
Whilk grantit me sic perfite pulchritude.
I mak a vow, with humill observance,
Richt reverently thy temple to visie
With sacrifice unto thy deitie!
To every state I am sa agreabill
That few or nane refuses me at all –
Papes, patriarchs, nor prelates venerabill,
Common people, nor princes temporal,
But subject all to me Dame Sensual!

(*celsitude* majesty)

This is John the Commonweal's complaint of the vicar appropriating the few possessions of the poor. The tone is much more colloquial, and noticeably in this passage, very close to contemporary spoken Scots:

> The poor cottar being like to die,
> Havand small bairnis twa or three,
> And has twa kye withouten mae,
> The vicar must have ane of thae,
> With the grey coat that haps the bed,
> Howbeit the wife be poorly cled!
> And if the wife die on the morn,
> Thocht all the bairns sould be forlorn,
> The other cow he cleeks away,
> With the poor coat of raploch grey.
> Wald god this custom was put doun
> Whilk never was foundit by reasoun!

> (*raploch* rough cloth)

For Lyndsay, tutor to James V, the relationship with his royal patron began in the King's infancy. One of his poems recalls the prince playing as a child, and the delight of the poet when his name was among the first sounds the infant uttered:

> How, as ane chapman beris his pak,
> I bure thy grace upon my bak,
> And sumtymes, strydlingis on my nek,
> Dansand with mony bend and bek.
> The first syllabis that thou did mute
> Was PA, DA LYN. Upon the lute
> Then playit I twenty spryngis.

> (*bek* bow)

Both Dunbar and Lyndsay were professional poets, supported by their positions at Court. Both depict the pleasures and passtimes of Court life.

Lyndsay:

> Off lustie lordis and lufesum ladyis ying,
> Tryumpand tornayis, iustyng, and knychtly game,
> With all pastyme accordyng for ane kyng.

Dunbar:

> Sum singis, sum dances, sum tellis storyis,
> Sum lait at evin bringis in the moryis.

The reign of James IV in particular was one of great achievement in Scottish culture. The Education Act of 1496 required elder sons of barons and substantial freeholders to master Latin and to undertake courses of study in arts and law. This led to a great improvement in regional administration. Scotland's third university, King's College Aberdeen was founded, giving the country one more seat of higher learning than her wealthier neighbour England. A programme of building was undertaken, influenced by French architects and master masons, who made the Great Hall of Stirling castle the first Renaissance construction in Scotland. The Chapel Royal was created at Stirling and one of its effects was to promote Musyck Fyne, as courtly music was termed. In Edinburgh, Chepman and Myllar set up the first printing presses. The status and popularity of the national poetry was confirmed when they published a collection by Henryson and Dunbar in 1509, the very first book to come off a Scottish printing press. A typical Renaissance prince, James encouraged those around him with his love for poetry, architecture, languages, and music, bringing foreign artists to settle in Scotland in order to diversify the cultural life of his Court. All of this was combined with an impetuous streak which would eventually lead to his ill-starred invasion of England and death at Flodden Field in 1513. Dunbar was one of the many recipients of James's bounty, but the court makar had a guid conceit of his abilities and resented sharing the king's patronage with all the foreign "mercenaries" at court:

> Soukaris, groukaris, gledaris gunnaris
> Monsouris of France, gud claret cunnaris,
> Inopportoun askaris of Yrland kynd,
> And meit revaris lyk out of mynd

> (*groukar* meaning unknown; *gledaris* mean folk; *cunnaris* tasters)

The close relationship the poet must have enjoyed with the King is revealed in the familiar way he is addressed by the poet, who is not scared to come straight to the point when the point is the poet's lack of ready cash:

> I haif inquyrit in mony a place,
> For help and confort in this cace,
> And all men sayis, My Lord that ye

> Can best remeid for this malice,
> That with sic panis prickillis me.

Dunbar would have been distinctly ill at ease if he had live through the reign of James V, as "Monsouris of France" and their culture gained even more prestige and patronage at court. James V married two Frenchwomen, the unfortunate Madeleine de Valois, who died soon after her arrival in Edinburgh, and Marie de Guise, who survived her husband and wielded tremendous pro-French political influence in the years leading up to the Reformation, as Regent for her daughter Mary, Queen of Scots. Mary married the Dauphin of France and was Queen of France during his brief reign as François III. There were many French settlers in Scotland at this time and some of them formed a colony in Little France on the outskirts of Edinburgh, an overspill from Craigmillar Castle. More French words were added to the already considerable stock in the language: *vivers* (provisions), *fash* (bother), *dote* (endow). The period was one of comparative prosperity for Scotland, but for many the French influence was regarded as extravagant in a country whose people had had to be frugal for most of their long history. Bishop Leslie, writing in 1537, was to be echoed more and more vociferously by the Protestant Reformers as the century wore on.

> There wes mony new ingynis and devysis, alsweill of bigging of palaces, abilyementis and of banquating, as of men's behaviour, first begun and usit in Scotland at this tyme, eftir the fassioune quhilk they had sene in France. Albeit it semit to be very comlie and beautiful, yit it was moir superfluous and voluptuous nor the substance of the realme of Scotland mycht beir furth or sustaine . . . . [and] remains yit to thir dayis, to the greit hinder and povertie of the hole realme.

(*bigging* building; *abilyementis* fashions, clothes)

The court poets had fewer qualms about the extravagance, provided they were part of it. Sir David Lyndsay's favourite place for enjoying the pleasures of court was Linlithgow.

> Lithgow, whose palyce of pleasaunce
> mycht be ane pattern in Portingale or Fraunce.

But the Court did not simply indulge itself in continental excess, for there, the Scottish poets absorbed influences from the other great literary languages of Europe. Villon of France, Ariosto of Italy and Chaucer of England were just a few of the writers whose marks can be traced in the work of the Middle Scots makars. In addition, as I have already indicated, classical Greek and especially Latin literature was profoundly influential not only on the theme and styles of the poetry but in the language the poets used. Latin was the language of international learning, the lingua franca of universities all over Europe. Later in the 16th century, Scotland produced in George Buchanan the greatest Latin writer in the Europe of the day. I say this to stress that the Scottish literati of the 16th century were part of a European world picture, intellectuals who read several languages and their literatures, and took what they wanted from the diverse sources available to them. Many today, however, can only approach the past from within the confines of the present totally different Scottish relationship with the world, and because of that, draw erroneous conclusions from the writings of the makars. This is especially noticeable in the area concerned with the relationship between Scots and English literature and language. Because Scottish culture has little status in Scotland and the U.K. today, many presume it has always been a provincial backwater, looking over its shoulder with envy to the glittering culture of the south. This attitude has also been fostered by the imperialism of English medievalist critics who, rather than admit to the superior worth of the Scots makars, simply appropriated them and relegated them with the ludicrous term Scottish Chaucerians!

As the father of poetry in the vernacular, as opposed to Latin, Chaucer was indeed revered by all of the makars. Dunbar's lines are typical:

> O reverend Chaucere, rose of rethoris all,
> As in oure tong ane flour imperiall . . .

Chaucer's prestige was such that the makars introduced English forms into certain styles of their verse, e.g. quho for quha, moste for maist, frome for fra, a fashion which increased dramatically after the Reformation. But in pre-Reformation Scotland there was never a slavish copying of English models, the native tradition was too vital and wide-ranging to draw from just one tradition. Indeed if one tradition dominated Scots literature, it was the Latin, not the English one. Dunbar's description of Chaucer as Rose of Rhetoric reminds us of the prestige of the Latin rhetoricians, and Dunbar applauds Chaucer's attempt to raise the vernacular up to the exalted standards of the classical language. This has to be remembered when you read the Scots poets apologising for the inadequacy of their language, and the necessity of extending it with words from other tongues. This is Gavin Douglas in the prologue to the first book of his Aeneid.

> And yit forsuyth I set my bissy pane
> As that I couth to mak it braid and plane,
> kepand na sudron bot our awyn langage,
> And spekis as I lernyt quhen I was page.
> Nor yit sa cleyn all sudron I refus,
> Bot sum word I pronunce as nyghtbouris doys:
> Lyke as in Latyn beyn Grew termys sum,
> So me behufyt quhilum or than be dum
> Sum bastard Latyn, French or Inglys oys
> Quhar scant was Scottis – I had nane other choys.

(*Grew* Greek; *quhilum* sometimes)

Many reading those lines today interpret them from the contemporary standpoint of regarding Scots as an inadequate bastardised dialect of English, and presume Douglas is admitting much the same there. In fact what he is doing is employing the rhetorical device, with which every vernacular writer in Europe preceded his work; an apology for the "rudeness" and "barbarity" of their tongue compared to others, especially Latin. This is Chaucer in the Prologue of the Franklin's Tale.

> At my bigynning first I yow biseche
> Have me excused of my rude speche
> I lerned nevere rethorik, certeyn;
> Thyng that I speke, it moot be bare and pleyn.

Writers using the English language throughout the 16th century are extremely disparaging as to its potential for eloquence, indeed so virulent are some of the epithets describing English's inadequacy that it would appear that the writers are not simply repeating parrot fashion the rhetorical disparagement, like, for example, their Scottish counterparts, but are actually expressing a deeply-felt belief as to the impoverished state of their language compared to others. In the midst of a paean of praise for all things English compared with all things foreign, *The fyrst boke of the Introduction of knowledge* puts a stop to the list at the subject of language:

> The speche of Englande is a base speche to other noble speches, as Italion, Castylion, and Frenche.

Throughout the 16th century English writers have few good words to say about their language, and it is only towards the latter part of the century that they begin to have grudging praise for the extension of its potential due to copious borrowing from Latin, Greek or French. Yet the same writers are aware that by the use of foreign terms, they are cutting off the majority of the population from comprehension of their native literature. Most carry on with the borrowings, however, in the hope that eventually the borrowed words will be absorbed into the everyday vocabulary of the people. In *The Arte of English Poesie*, written in 1589 by George Puttenham, the author discusses the fashion for borrowing and the possible detrimental effect it could have. He fears it will leave English a hotchpotch or as he terms it, a "mingle mangle" which occurs, "when we make our speache or writinges of sundry languages using some Italian word, or French, or Spanish, or Dutch, or Scottish, not for the nonce or for any purpose (which were in part excusable) but ignorantly and affectedly".

A possible explanation for the inferioriy complex Englishmen undoubtedly had regarding their mother tongue lies in the fact that historically it had to contend not only with the prestigious classical languages for status, but also with another European vernacular language, French. The Norman invasion in the 11th century had made French the language of the English royal court, the law, the prestigious register of the aristocracy, and of a thriving Anglo-Norman literature. John Gower (1330-1408), for example, is hailed as one of the early exponents of English for literary purposes, but much of his best work, the *Balades* were written in French. In the 14th century Robert of Gloucester stated that for a man to be highly regarded in

England, he had to speak French. To all intents and purposes, for over two centuries, English was regarded as the dialect of the lower classes, and it was only after Chaucer had proved that it was capable of being a great literary tongue, that its low status slowly changed. By the end of the 15th century, William Caxton apologises not only for his "rude and comyn englyshe", with its lack of ornate eloquence, but for his imperfect knowledge of French, which renders his translations from the noble French tongue doubly barbaric. For long after French ceased as an everyday language in England, it continued alongside Latin as the preferred language of, for example, education, parliamentary and local records, and the law. Only after 1450 do we see most English towns changing over from French to English for recording their public transactions. Law French in fact continued to be used in England until the Revolution of 1688, by which time it was very much a debased jargon, with its practitioners divorced from a real grasp of the language. A report on a trial of 1631 for example could have come out of Punch's Franglais column; there a prisoner is described losing his temper with the judge, and proceding to "jecte un graund brickbat que narrowly mist"!!

The contrast with the Scottish situation is striking. In the period when the English of England was at its lowest ebb and Norman French in the ascendancy – from the late 11th century to the early 14th century – the Inglis of Scotland was engaged in its triumphant rise all over the Lowlands, to become the language of court and state. In Scotland, the Anglo-Norman nobility appear to have deserted their French for Inglis much earlier than in England, so that while French had prestige, it showed itself in the borrowings it gave to Scots, rather than setting itelf up as an alternative to Scots. Latin was the only serious contender to Scots in matters concerning high culture in Scotland, while in England both Latin and French were regarded as more prestigious languages than the native English. I have been looking at the status of English in England in order to compare it with Scots in Scotland in the 16th century, and give the general European background to feelings about vernacular languages versus Latin and Greek. This I feel is necessary to balance the world picture of the modern reader, who has been conditioned to presume that English always had prestige, and Scots never had it, which is patently not the case during the Golden Age of Scottish culture in the reigns of James IV and V.

When Gavin Douglas augments his Scots with Latin, French and English, he is part of a European phenomenon, as were the English writers who supplemented their language by the same borrowings, and with the same misgivings about its comprehensibility to the ordinary folk. Douglas is adamant to stress that Scottis is "skant", not in relation to English, which is how many interpret his statement today, but in relation to the style of Virgil's poetry. His language lacks the colours of rhetoric, the sentence, and gravity of the original.

> Nocht for our tong is in the selwyn skant
> Bot for that I the fowth of language want
> Quhar as the cullour of his properte
> To kepe the sentence tharto constrenyt me . . .

> (*in the selwyn* in itself; *fowth* abundance; *properte* purport, meaning)

Shortly after this conventional statement of modesty, Douglas goes on to show that he in fact has a guid conceit of his ability to use language as a poetic craftsman, and turns on what he considers to be the pathetic attempts by William Caxton to translate Virgil into English.

> Thocht Wilyame Caxtoun, of Inglis natioun,
> In proys hes prent ane buke of Inglys gross,
> Clepand it Virgill in Eneados,
> Quhilk that he says of Franch he dyd translait,
> It has na thing ado tharwith, God wait . . . .
> So schamefully that story dyd pervert.
> I red his wark with harmys at my hert,
> That syk a buke but sentens or engyne
> Suld be intitillit eftir the poet dyvyne;
> Hys ornate goldyn versis mair than gilt
> I spittit for dispyte to se swa spilt
> With sych a wyght, quhilk trewly be myne intent
> Knew never thre wordis at all quhat Virgill ment . . .

> (*but sentens or engyne* without eloquence or ingenuity; *wyght* man)

This is not the tone of one seeking models of excellence in English language and letters. The relationship between Scots and English culture of the 15th and 16th centuries was the relationship of equals, with the Scots praising or criticising, borrowing or slandering where they saw fit. If Henryson and James I owed a poetical debt to Chaucer, the same was the case with Skelton and Surrey, to Dunbar and Douglas. For both nations' poets at this time, the native tradition in either country was much more influential to the development of their art than what was going on North or South of a distant border. Modern critics' constant comparison with English culture obscures the European dimension the Scots makars were working within, and reduces it to the inappropriate limitations of the British scenario which many cannot see beyond.

The unknown author of *The Complaynt of Scotland* (1548) more typically discusses the use of language purely in terms of the advantages and disadvantages of using Scots as opposed to Latin. He addresses himself to the intellectuals of the country with conventional humility, asking them to excuse the poverty of the writing by remembering the patriotic intent behind the work.

> . . . that procedis fra ane affectiue ardant fauoir that I hef euyr borne touart this affligit realme quhilk is my natiue cuntre. Nou heir i exort al philosophouris, historiographours, & oratours of our scottis natione to support & til excuse my barbir agrest termis; For I thocht it not necessair til haf fardit and lardit this tracteit with exquisite termis, quhilkis ar nocht daly usit, bot rather I hef usit domestic Scottis langage, maist intelligibil for the vlgar pepil.

(*agrest* rural; *fardit* embellished)

The author goes on to ridicule the "glorius consaits" of past authors, who showed off by using "thir lang tailit vordis" such as conturbabuntur or innumerabilibus. While criticising verbal extravagance for extravagance sake, like Douglas and other European vernacular writers, he is aware that Latin has such a range of rhetorical devices, that it is difficult to find equivalents in Scots.

> Ther for it is necessair at sum tyme til myxt oure langage vitht part of termis dreuin fra lateen, be rason that oure scottis tong is nocht sa copeus as in the lateen tong, ande alse ther is diuerse purposis & propositions that occurris in the latyn tong that can nocht be translatit deuly in oure scottis langage: therfor

> he that is expert in latyn tong suld nocht put reproche to the compilation, quhou beit that he fynd sum purposis translatit in scottis that accords nocht vitht the latyn register: as ve hef exempil of this propositione, homo est animal. for this term homo signifeis baytht man ande voman, bot ther is nocht ane scottis terme that signifeis baytht man and voman.

The author goes on to give other examples where he has kept the original word, rather than change the meaning of it by giving a Scots word which does not translate the concept exactly. He concludes the Prolog to the Redar by reiterating his earlier statement that he is writing not for vainglory, but "public necessite". The book itself consists mainly of translations and adaptations into Scots, mainly from French sources, in particular Alain Chartier's *Quadrilogue Invectif*. Through the character of Dame Scotia, the author's *Complaynt* is aimed directly against English meddling in Scottish affairs, and as we shall see, he fairly gets going when his dander is up. But the author and Dame Scotia are at their best when the intent is not propogandist, but penetrating asides such as this eternal feminist truth.

> Ane man is nocht reput for ane gentil man in Scotland bot gyf he mak mair expensis on his horse and his doggis nor he dois on his vyfe and bayrnis.

There are also a few passages which are strikingly original and rooted in a natural depiction of the Scottish environment. One of these involves a scene where country folk gather and have a party detailing the kinds of songs, stories, music and dance popular in mid 16th century Scotland. Another scene paints a vivid picture of not only the birds and animals which throng the countryside, but also attempts to reproduce exactly the sounds that they make, employing the old Scots alliterative tradition to good effect. Here is a short extract:

> The ropeen of the ravynis gart the cran crope, the huddit crauis cryit varrok, varrok, quhen the suannis murnit, because the gray goul mau pronosticat ane storme. The turtil began for to greit, quhen the cuschet youlit. the titlene follouit the gouk, and gart her sing guk, guk. The dou croutit hyr sad sang that soundit lyk sorrow . . . the laverok maid melody up hie in the skyis.

(*goul mau* seagull; *cuschet* wood pigeon; *titlene* meadow pipit; *gouk* cuckoo; *dou* dove; *laverok* lark)

Nevertheless, no prose writer in Scots in this period ever achieved the brilliance of the makars in poetry. In the Middle Ages and Renaissance, creative imaginative writing tended to be confined to poetry. Prose dominated the realm of practical information to be communicated in as straightforward a manner as possible. Local and national records, Acts of Parliament, the law and accounts of trials were the main uses for vernacular prose. From the mid 15th century on, however, there appear translations from Latin and French sources and original works of a more creative nature, though their aim is usually didactic: Sir Gilbert Hay's *The Buke of the Law of Armys*, and John of Ireland's *The Meroure of Wysdome* are typically solid but uninspired examples. As writers turned more and more to the vernacular rather than Latin for serious writing, the style of Scots prose gradually progressed. John Bellenden's Scots translation of Hector Boece's *Chronicles of Scotland* in 1531 was the first of a vigorous tradition of Scots historical writing, continued later on in the century by such as Robert Lyndesay of Pitscottie, and Father James Dalrymple, the translator of Bishop Leslie's ten-volume Latin *History of Scotland*. Shakespeare did not have to stretch his imagination overmuch – the third scene in Act I of Macbeth came to him through Holinshed's English version of Bellenden's Scots:

Quhen Makbeth and Banquho war passand to Fores, quhair King Duncan wes for the tyme thai mett be the gaitt thre weird sisteris or wiches, quhilk, come to thame with elrege clething. The first of thame sayid to Makbeth: "Haill, Thayne of Glammys!" the secund sayid: "Haill, Thayn of Cawder!" The thrid sayid: "Haill, Makbeth, that salbe sum tyme King of Scotland!" Than said Banquho: "Quhat wemen be ye, quhilkis bene sa unmercifull to me and sa propiciant to my companyeoun, gevand him nocht onlie landis and grete rentis bot als triumphand kingdome, and gevis me nocht". To this ansuerit the first of thir witches: "We schaw mair feliciteis appering to the than to him; for thocht he happin to be ane king, yit his empyre sall end unhappely, and nane of his blude sall eftir him succede. Be contrair, thou sal neuer be king, bot of the sall cum mony kingis, quhilkis with land and anciant lynage sall reioise the croun of Scotland." Thir wourdis beand sayid, thai suddanlye evanyst oute of thair sycht.

One of the most interesting works of the age follows the conventional format of a wise older man giving sound moral advice to a younger man. But in Maister Myll's "Spektakle of Luf", written in St Andrews in 1492, there is more than a suggestion that the author wanted to titillate his audience as well as instructing them against the sin of extramarital sex. The book, re-published in the Bannatyne Miscellany in the 19th century, is divided into chapters which contain examples from classical history which the father hopes will convince his son to avoid variously the "delectatioun of . . . . damesillis or young wemen . . . . uther mennis wyffis . . . . wedowis and agit wemen. . . . and (last but certainly not least) . . . . The sevynt part schawis that men suld forbeir the delectatioun of wemen of religioun, as nunnis or utheris, with gret examplis allegit tharapon"! The boy originally thinks there could be little harm in the occasional dalliance with any of the women on faither's list, but faither soon disabuses him of any such notions. Just one of the numerous stories on wedowis and ancient wemen should be enough to convince any wayward son that celibacy is the only safe existence.

> My Sone, has thow nocht hard that the Quene of Navarre duelt and had hyr mansioun within the toun of Parys, apon the wattir syd of Sayne. This Quene was sa lechorus, that scho desyrit of euery plesand man to have assaye, and sa covatys, that scho wald tak lay meid and proffet tharfor; for the quhilk, als sone as thai had done with hyr at thai mycht, scho wald tak fra thame all thar reches, and a trap within hir chalmer, that was abone the watter, thai war lattyn fall doun, quhar thai war drownyt. And thus mony noble men war myssit, bot nane cuth juge be quhat waye; be the quhilk this Quene grew to sa gret reches of gold that it was mervall, quhill the clerk Prudane persavit this trap, quhar he ordanit his servandis to be in a boit. On the nycht he passit to the Quenis chalmer, and lay with hir to his plesour, and payet the monye; and quhen he had done, he was pelit and cassyn doun at the trap as utheris was done of befor, quhar his servandis in the boite keppit him sone . . . .

> (*meid* reward; *quhill* until; *pelit* robbed)

If medieval Scots prose had few outstanding figures, it did function well in its role of keeper of the nation's records. Public records are not the place for stylists to exhibit their rhetorical skills, but often realistic portrayals of actual events provide humorous pictures of our ancestors. The following dialogue could be from the "Little Stories from the Police Courts" column in D.C. Thomson's *Weekly News,* but in fact they are from a trial recorded in the Kirk Session records of St Andrews in 1560:

> "My brother is and salbe vicar of Crayll quhen thow sal thyg thy mait, fals smayk; I sall pul the owt of the pulpot be the luggis and chais the owt of this town".

> "It is schame to yow that ar gentillmen that ye pull hym nocht owt of the pulpot be the luggis."

> (*thyg* beg; *mait* meat; *smayk* rogue; *luggis* ears)

Similarly evocative of the language and the period are the countless inscriptions which adorn the buildings in the old burghs. Many are of a pious nature, such as the following from the Old Town of Edinburgh:

HE. YT. THOLIS. OVERCUMMIS.

O. LORD. IN. THE. IS. AL. MY. TRAIST.

LUFE. GOD. ABUFE. AL. AN. THY. NYCHTBOUR. AS. THY. SELF

The latter can still be seen carved in gold outside the house where John Knox is supposed to have lived in the High Street. Other inscriptions are pithy epigrammatic sayings, such as the one gracing the house in Dunfermline at 21 Marygate:

SENN WORD IS THRALL AND THOCHT IS FRE KEIP WEILL THY TONGE I COINSELL THE.

The official government and royal records are again more interesting for the political and historical information they contain than for their use of Scots. But as language was profoundly affected by politics, particularly religious politics in the second half of the 16th century, the Acts of Parliament take on greater significance for the history of Scots. The following is a short extract from an act of Marie de Guise in 1558, naturalising French citizens living in Scotland.

> Because the maist Christian King of France has granted ane
> letter of naturalitie for him and his successors to all and sundrie
> Scotsmen – registered in the Chalmer of Compts – therefore
> the Queen's Grace, Dowager and Regent of this Realme and
> the three Estaitis of the samin thinks it guid and agreeable that
> the like letter of naruralitie be given and granted by the King
> and Queen of Scotland.

Writers of prose in Scots, like the makars with their poetic
flyting tradition, often appear to derive inspiration from the
opportunity to rail against something. One of the favourite
targets then as now, and with much more justification, was the
English. English culture was admired north of the Border, but
the English nation in general was regarded with an hostility
born of centuries of distrust and warfare. The author of *The
Complaynt of Scotland*, a committed supporter of the Catholic
and French faction in Scottish affairs, is nowhere more articulate
than when he is giein the English laldy.

> Inglis men ar humil quhen thai ar subjeckit be forse and violence,
> and Scottis men ar furious quhen thai ar violently subjeckit.
> Inglismen ar cruel quhene thai get victorie, and Scottis men ar
> merciful quhen thai get victorie. And to conclude, it is onpossibil
> that Scottis men and Inglis men can remane in concord undir
> ane monarch or ane prince, because there naturis and conditions
> ar as indifferent as is the nature of scheip and volvis.

There may be a degree of exaggeration in the analogy of the
two peoples being as different as sheep and wolves. But in the
aftermath of the Reformation we shall see that as far as the
Scots and English languages are concerned the analogy is not
so far fetched.

# Chapter 4

## Two Diadems in One

Stewart Scots and Tudor English enjoyed the same kind of relationship as Dutch and German, Portuguese and Spanish, or Danish and Swedish today. In other words, Scots and English were dialects arising from a common root which developed independently due to political, rather than linguistic factors. Educated men or women from either country could read the other's language with reasonable ease, though the spoken tongue presented far greater, but not insurmountable difficulties. People who commented on the languages could emphasise their differences or their similarities, depending on which political purpose it suited. In the period of the Reformation politics were polarised into two major factions, and both had good reason to adopt a partisan attitude to one or other view of the languages.

The reforming party in Scotland had always been close to the Reformers in England, and looked south for political help against the Catholic pro-French faction in Scotland. Closer political union with England, they felt, would guarantee the Protestant ascendancy. When Knox and his co-religionists succeeded in establishing Presbyterianism, no complete translation of the Bible into Scots existed. This meant that the first non-Latin Bible available was the Geneva English edition. This was seized upon and came to exercise a tremendous influence on a country besotted with religion. From then on God spoke English. The Catholic party railed at the anglophile tendencies among the protestant propagandists, citing their desertion of their native tongue as particularly deplorable. In John Knox, they had a fair target, for the father figure of Reformation in Scotland was exceptionally anglicised in his writing for that age. For whatever reasons – his long spells abroad, his stays in England, political motivation to bring Scots closer to England in language as well as religion, or simply personal predilection. Knox is the first known Scot in history to attempt to conform his writing to English models. The Catholic Ninian Wynyet, writing from the safety of Paris, it should be noted, tries to get at Knox by citing his aping of English fashion:

> Gif ye, throw curiositie of novatiounis, hes foryet our auld plane Scottis quhilk your mother leirit you, in tymes coming I sall wryte to you my mind in Latin for I am nocht acquent with your Suddrone.

That is very much an ironic dig at the Reformer, not to be taken too literally. But, another of the counter-Reformers, William Hamilton, was even more vitriolic in his criticism:

> Giff King James the fyft war alyve, quha hering ane of his subjectis knap suddrone, declarit him ane trateur: quidder vald he declaire you triple traitoris, quha not onlie knappis suddrone in your negative confession, bot also hes causit it to be imprentit in London in contempt of our native language.

(*knap suddrone* speak English)

There is no trace of James V putting anyone to death for knappin suddrone, and Hamilton is undoubtedly exaggerating to make a dramatic point in his argument. The fact remains though that these Catholics had a genuine grievance in that the Protestants were initiating a process whereby gradually the English option was preferred to the Scottish one in writing, or more exactly, printing.

The Reformers are often blamed erroneously for the demise of Scots, because they adopted an English Bible and Psalm Book. It must be stressed, however, that their aims were religious rather than linguistic. Historical accident and the human expediency of a readily-available English Bible were more important than any pro-Scots or pro-English linguistic identity among the Protestants. In the context of the 16th century it was not necessary for Scots to define the linguistic community they belonged to, and this is another reason why, when English came in, it found little national resistance. The vernacular could be called either Scottis or Inglis, and the choice of term seems to have been arbitrary – they were often used synonomously for the vernacular of Lowland Scotland.

An Act of Parliament of 1542 allowing the use of a vernacular Bible states:

> . . . it salbe lefull to all our souirane ladyis lieges to haif the haly write baith the new testament and the auld in the vulgar toung in Inglis or scottis of ane gude and trew translatioun and that thai incur no crimes for the hefin or reding of the samin.

This could be interpreted as meaning either a Scots or an English version, recognising the differences between the languages, but not caring which one is taken up as long as it is in a vernacular the people can understand. But more than likely it simply means that the terms were interchangeable. The English Bible existed through the quirk of fate that the Reformers in England were ahead of the Scots because of Henry VIII's rift with Rome over his marriage problems. Henry desperately wanted a Protestant ally on his northern Border, and knew of the growing clamour there for the new teaching. His envoy in Scotland told him in the early 1540s of the demand for vernacular Bibles and psalters with the words, "if a cartlode [were] sent thither they wolde be bought, every one". That some of them did get there and were instrumental in fomenting a radical critique of the Church is testified in Lyndsay's *Ane Satyre of the Thre Estaitis*, first performed around the year 1540. In one scene, the revelry of the Vices is interrupted by the arrival of Veritie, carrying her Bible. Flatterie is horrified:

> What buik is that, harlot, into thy hand?
> Out! Walloway! This is the New Test'ment,
> In Englisch toung, and printit in England!
> Herisie! Herisie! fire! fire! incontinent.

> (*incontinent* immediately)

Veritie is fortunately not burned as a heretic, as Flatterie would like, but Truth is nevertheless temporarily suppressed when Veritie is put in the stocks. The feeling abroad in Scotland was that a vernacular Bible was urgently required, and it little mattered in which of the national vernaculars, Stewart Scots, or Tudor English, it came.

Another feature arising out of the similarities in the two written languages, is that Scots could read a text in English, yet translate it into their own idiom when speaking it. Thus

English could be adapted to Scots, so even those with an identity for the national language could accept English texts, knowing they would Scotticise them for public utterance. A modern parallel may clarify the situation further. Lewis Grassic Gibbon's novel *Sunset Song* can be read as Standard English, and that partly explains the novel's success with non-Scottish readers. However for those from a Scots-speaking background, it can be rendered broad Scots by simply changing the pronunciation and intonation of the English text. So it must have been with Scots reading the English biblical texts at the time of Reformation.

There is evidence also that at the time of Reformation, Scots scribes or printers would often reset an English text into a Scots version, based on the way they would pronounce the words themselves. Mairi Robinson, Editor-in-chief of *The Concise Scots Dictionary,* has made a detailed examination of the language used in various editions of The Scots Confession of 1560 – "one of the few indigenous documents of the Reformation in Scotland". The source of the Confession is English, probably Tyndale's New Testament which had been circulating in Scotland since 1526. The various manuscript editions of the Confession, however, adapt the text to more common Scottish features – e.g. quhilk for which, gif for if, lang for long, and past tenses ending in –it rather than –ed. Here are examples of the alterations, the first is from Tyndale's original, the second from one of the most Scots of the various manuscripts.

> And this glad tidingees of the kyngdome shal be preached in all the worlde for a witnes unto all nacions: and then shall the ende come.

> And this glaid tydingis of the kyngdome sall be precheit throwch the haill warld for a witnes unto all natiouns, and than sall the end cum

One of the manuscripts was completed twenty years after the first Confession, but there too there was still no evidence of the scribe going more for the English option available – his text has a similar degree of anglicisation of style or scotticisation of English as his predecessor's. This again indicates that the Protestants had no policy of standardising their texts towards

English models. Similarly, with the printed editions, the normal Scots state of affairs in the 16th century, with wide variation in spelling conventions seems to prevail, rather than the more standardised spelling of the English printing of the period. Robinson suggests that one of the principle printers anglicises his printing of the Confession not through intent, but through ignorance of the Scots orthographic conventions. When he came back to Scotland, Robert Lekpreuik was a novice in printing in Scots and so abided by the more familiar English models. A few years later, however, he is printing the Acts of Parliament in the correct Scots of the day. If the Reformers had adopted an active policy against Scots, this would have been increasingly reflected in the work of their official printer. That it is not, strengthens the thesis that the anglicisation was part of a wider process, but a process which was undoubtedly precipitated by the adoption of an English Bible.

Strengthening the process was the fact that England was the source of the vast majority of printed books available in Scotland. The few Scottish printing presses in existence copied the technique and language from the English works available as models. The importance of the Bible and the concomitant rise in prestige that English enjoyed, resulted in what was initially a slow adaptation of Scots to English in printing becoming a rapid pre-eminence of English over Scots. Thus the final printed edition of the Confession of the 16th century – Skene's edition of 1597 – is much more English in style than previous printings of the work. Market forces came into play as well, with Scots printers realising that if they anglicised their texts they could appeal to the much bigger English public. None of this could have happened however if the written languages had not been so similar to start with. Indeed the process of anglicisation is much older than the Reformation, with the makars introducing English forms to increase their linguisitic options in their poetry, in the same way that Burns would rhyme Scots and English words much later, in the 18th century.

Of course, it could all have been very different. Protestant writing and parts of a New Testament in Scots had been in existence for a good half century before the triumph of the Reformers. Over thirty Lollard dissenters were tried in Ayrshire in 1494, and it was a member of that sect, Murdoch Nisbet from Newmilns in my own Irvine Valley, who translated parts of

Wycliffe's New Testament into Scots around 1528. This passage is from Matthew 10. and describes Jesus performing miracles.

> And, lo, a woman that had the bludy flux xii yere, neirit behind, and tuichet the hemm of his clathe: for scho said within herself, gif I tuiche anly the clathe of him, I salbe saif. and Jesus turnyt and sau hir and said "Douchtir, have thou traist; thi faith has made the saif." And the woman was hale fra that hour.

Unfortunately the Nisbet version remained in manuscript form during the crucial period. If it had been printed it may have acted as a catalyst for a complete Scots Bible. One of the earliest Scottish statements of the Protestant doctrine was published in Malmø in 1533 by John Gau, a former student of St Andews who had to leave Scotland because of his heretical opinions. There is no hint of an anglicised Reformation in his vigorously Scots rendering of the Creed.

> I trou in God fader almichtine, maker of heuine and yeird, and in Jesu Christ his sone our onlie Lord, the quhilk wes consawit of the halie Spreit and born of Maria virginem he sufert onder Poncio Pilat to be crucifeit to de and to be yeirdit; he descendit to the hel, and rais fra deid the thrid day; he ascendit to the heuine, and sittis at almichtine God the fader's richt hand; he is to cum agane to juge quyk and deid; I trou in the halie spreit; I trow that thair is one halie chrissine kirk and ane communione of sanctis; I trou forgiffine of sinis; I trou the resurrectione of the flesch; I trou the euerlastand liff.

> (*yeirdit* buried)

The book, based on the work of a Danish Reformer called Christiern Pedersen is entitled, *The Richt Vay to the Kingdom of Heuine*. In his introduction the author is precise as to who the book is for, and what they will learn from it.

> The richt and chrissine doctrine is heir contenit in this present buyk that al quhilk onderstandis the scotis tung ma haiff with thayme and reid and usz it dailie. That thay may chrissinlie leir and onderstand first quhou thay sall ken thair sins and ar sinful creatures. this thay suld leir of the x commandis of God.

Gau is a Protestant addressing his fellow-countrymen in their national language, and there he is using the term Scots, in the sense that we know it today, differentiating it from the Inglis of England. A similar use is found in An Act of the Lords of Council of 1534, possibly referring to Gau's book. It outlines the sources of the heretical vernacular works coming into Scotland.

> Thir new bukis maid be the said Lutheris secteis baith in Latyne, Scottis, Inglis and Flemys.

The differences between the languages were such that even the revered English poets, Chaucer, Lydgate and countless unknown authors, rarely appeared in Scottish manuscripts or even early printed books in their original English form. The common practise was to render them Scots for the Scots reading public. The changes in spelling could be easily effected by scribes.

But if the differences in the written languages were rarely commented upon, that is not the case with the spoken tongues. There, the differences were more obvious. Pedro de Ayala was not the only foreigner to recognise that Scots and English were distinct languages. The Magistrates of Stockholm as late as 1680 employed one Will Guthrie as interpreter for the English and Scottish tongues. Two Scottish monarchs, separated by over 150 years, pass comment on the foreignness of the English of England. It is recorded in the Scotichronicon that the young James I in the early years of his captivity at the English court (1406-1424) found it difficult to decipher a tongue he had never heard before; "etsi linguam quam non noverat audivit". Mary, Queen of Scots also refers to the difficulty of Scots and English communicating. When similarly imprisoned in England in 1581, she endeavoured to procure priests who would set about re-converting her son James VI to Catholicism. When she heard that two English Jesuits had been chosen for the task, she remonstrated both on account of the inbred animosity between the two peoples and revealingly, because, "they are foreigners and do not understand the language, they could not do much good." Mary is not just another Catholic exaggerating the differences for rhetorical effect. She passionately cared for the work the priests were chosen to do, but realised that they did not possess the necessary linguistic apparatus to carry it out. Scots and English could be regarded as different dialects of the same language, but where sensitivity and painstaking negotiation was required the differences between the two languages was obviously more crucial than their surface similarities.

Of course, it is only now, long after the event, that we can analyse a subject like language change with any degree of objectivity. When the anglicisation of the Scots tongue was beginning through readings from the English Bible, very few people were aware that such a process was in fact taking place. For the majority of course it was not taking place – they lived and died monoglot Scots speakers. The fact that I, writing in 1986, was brought up with a full dialect of Scots as my first language, says much for the survival of a tongue, supposed to have been dealt a death blow in 1560.

In fact the period during and immediately following the Reformation was one of great richness in Scots language and literature. Printing flourished and a great diversity of books were published. The Register of the Privy Seal in 1559 lists the books published by William Nudrye, who was given the privilege of printing and distributing books authorised by the State.

> [Maister] William Nudry's Short Introduction Elementar, degestit into sevin breve taiblis for the commodious expeditioun of thame that are desirous to reid and write the Scottish tongue; Ane Instructioun for bairnis to be lernit in Scottis and Latene; Ane ABC for Scottis men to reid the French toung, with an exhortatioun to the noblis of Scotland to favour thair ald freinds.

It was worth people's while to master the written Scots of this period, for the disputatious side of the Scottish character was allowed full rein in the intense debate over the religious future of the nation, and the prose writing that arose was fired with commitment. Though sometimes alien to our modern sensibility, its native vigour is undiminished across the centuries. This is Knox's gleeful description of the murderers of Cardinal Beaton hanging his body over the wall of his castle at St Andrews to prove the deed to the crowd.

> And so was he brought to the East blokhouse head, and schawen dead ower the wall to the faythless multitude, which wold not beleve befoir it saw: How miserably lay David Betoun, cairfull Cardinall. And so thei departed without Requiem alternam,

and Requiescat in pace, song for his saule. Now, becaus the wether was hote (for it was in Maij, as ye have heard) and his funerallis could not suddandly be prepared, it was thowght best, to keap him frome styncking, to geve himn great salt ynewcht, a cope of lead, and a nuk in the boddome of the Sea-toure ( a place where many of Goddis childrene had bein empreasoned befoir) to await what exequeis his brethrene the bischopps wold prepare for him.

These thingis we wreat merelie.

You will notice from comparing the language of Knox's *History of the Reformation* with the other writers of the age that the Reformer's style is much closer to English practice. But even he could jibe at someone who lacked a good command of Scots. Elsewhere in the *History,* he describes one of his enemies: "He nether had French nor Latyne, and some say his Scottishe toung was nott verray good". If an anglicised Knox comes as a surprise to those brought upon the myth of the man as the classic dour Scot, the description of his style of preaching by Mr James Melville, ties perfectly with the popular image. Melville's Diary of the years 1556-1601 gives superb insight into the life of the later 16th century. Here he recalls Knox at St Andrews

> . . . when he enterit to application, he maid me sa to grew and tremble that I could nocht hald a pen to wryt . . . I saw him everie day of his doctrine go hulie and fear, with a furring of martriks about his neck, a staff in the ane hand, and guid godly Richart Ballanden his seruand, haldin upe the uther oxter, from the Abbaye to the paroche Kirk, and be the said richart and another seruant lifted upe to the pulpit, whar he behovit to lean at his first entrie, bot, or he had done with his sermon, he was sa actiue and vigorus, that he was lyk to ding that pulpit in blads and flie out of it.

> (*grew* shudder with fear; *hulie and fear* warily; *martriks* pine marten [fur]; *ding in blads* smash to pieces)

The foremost historian of the day was Robert Lindesay of Pitscottie, near Cupar in Fife. His *Historie and Cronicles of Scotland* gives a lively account of events in the country between 1437 and 1575. Here is part of his account of the death of James V and the King hearing the news of the birth of Mary, Queen of Scots. It contains one of the famous sayings of Scottish history.

> Be this the post came out of Lythtgow schawing to the king
> good tydingis that the quene was deliuerit. The King inquyrit
> 'wither it was man or woman.' The messenger said 'it was ane
> fair douchter'. The king ansuerit and said: 'Adew, fair weill,
> it come witht ane lase, it will pase witht ane lase' . . . . He
> turnit him bak and luikit and beheld all his lordis about him
> and gaiff ane lytill smyle and lauchter, syne kyssit his hand
> and offerit the samyn to all his lordis round about him, and
> thairefter held upe his handis to God and yeildit the spreit.

Both the strengths and weaknesses of the position of Scots
as a national language which was gradually being undermined
by English is revealed in the writings of James VI. The gradual
anglicization of Scots can be seen in three editions of James'
book on royal statecraft, *The Basilicon Doron* (Kingly Gift), a
work originally hand-written in Scots in 1598. Within the space
of five years the language changes from Scots to English, and
phrases such as "tak narrow tent" are altered to "take narrow
heede" in printed editions. The first passage is from the original
manuscript, the second from the Waldegrave edition of 1603.

> . . . but as ye are cledd uith tua callings sa man ye be alyke
> cairfull for the dischairge of thaime baith, that as ye are a goode
> christiane sa ye maye be a goode king dischairging youre office
> as I sheu before in the pointis of iustice & equitie, quhilke in
> tua sindrie uayes ye man do . . .

> But as ye are clothed with two callings, so must ye be alike
> carefull for the discharge of them both: that as ye are a good
> Christian, so may ye be a good King, discharging your office (as
> I shewed before) in the points of justice and aequity: whiche
> in two sundry waies ye must doe . . . .

The change in the language reflected very much the way the
King himself was moving as far as culture and language was
concerned. After his Court moved to London, of course,
James showed little interest in Scotland or things Scottish, and
projected himself very much as a British King.

Before he left Scotland, however, he had been a great
champion of the Scots poetic tradition. In his teens he wrote
the first Scottish treatise on the theory of poetry entitled
*Ane Schort Treatise conteining some reulis and cautelis to be
obseruit and eschewit in Scottis Poesie*. In the preface he gives
as his reasons for undertaking the work the fact that most of

the books written are archaic, but also that the difference of language requires different techniques.

> The uther cause is, That as for thame that hes written of it of late, there hes never ane of them written in our language. for albeit sindrie hes written of it in English, quhilk is lykest to our language, yit we differ from thame in sindry reulis of Poesie.

His enthusiasm was not just a passing youthful phase and the last Scottish Court was one in which literature was patronised above all other arts. James's intent as stated in the *Reulis*, was to promote Scottish vernacular literature by modelling his school of poets on the Pléiade in France. The new Scottish poetry was to be thoroughly Scots, yet also completely European, James inviting poets from France and England such as Du Bellay, Du Bartas and Henry Constable to create the kind of creative intellectual exchange which would help the native muse thrive. The King himself was fluent in French, Italian and with teachers such as the great Buchanan his comment on his education is perhaps not surprising, "they gar me speik Latin ar I could speik Scotis." In the cosmopolitan environment of Edinburgh, he gathered around him an impressive group of writers which he termed his Castalian Band, including Alexander Montgomerie, John Stewart of Baldynneis, Alexander Hume, and Mark Alexander Boyd. All were gifted exponents of the native poetic tradition. In Alexander Montgomerie (1545?-1610?), the most important influence on the rest of the Band, we can recognise someone who is a direct heir of the tradition of Dunbar. The court poet of James VI, like his predecessor at the court of James IV, is concerned in his verse with social criticism, flyting with poetic adversaries, and constantly begging for his pension to be renewed by the King. This is him addressing the Lords of Session:

> My Lords, late lads, now leiders of our lauis,
> Except your gouns, some hes not worth a grote.
> Your colblack conscience all the countrey knawis;
> How can ye live, except ye sell your vote?

This is the opening verse of his flyting, or poetic slandering, with Patrick Hume of Polwart which harks back to Dunbar's famous flyting with Walter Kennedy.

Polwart, yee peip like a mouse amongst thornes;
Na cunning yee keepe; Polwart, yee peip;
Yee look like a sheipe, and yee had twa hornes:
Polwart, ye peip like a mouse amongst thornes.

Finally, here is part of his highly ornate plea to James to restore his patronage. This was written on Montgomerie's return to Scotland after imprisonment in England. James revered Montgomerie as a poet, recalling "His suggred stile his weightie words divine". But he was also wary of the poet's Catholic leanings in the charged atmosphere of post-Reformation Scotland. Montgomerie's pleading takes on a rather tragic note, when we know it was done in vain. The artificial "suggrit" aureate or high style in Scots would die a death when the Court moved south and the patronage for such poetry disappeared.

Help, Prince, to whom, on whom not, I complene
But on, not to, fals Fortun ay my fo
Quho but, not by, a resone reft me fro
Quho did, not does, yet suld my self sustene.
Of crymis, not cairs, since I haif kept me clene
I thole, not thanks, thame, sir, who served me so
Quha heght, not held, to me and mony mo
To help, not hurt, but hes not byding bene:
Sen will, not wit, too lait-whilk I lament –
Of sight, not service, shed me from your grace
With, not without, your warrand yit I went
In wryt, not words: the papers are in place.
Sen chance, not change, hes put me to this pane
Let richt, not reif, my pensioun bring agane.

(*heght* promised)

James would have been flattered and pleased by the poem, not just for the craftsmanship of its construction, but because it is in sonnet form, a form he personally did much to promote in Scotland.

One of the finest love poems in Scots, also a sonnet, was written at this time by Mark Alexander Boyd. A later member of the Castalian Band, everything else that remains of what he wrote is in Latin.

Fra banc to banc, fra wod to wod, I rin

Ourhailit with my feble fantasie,
Lyc til a leif that fallis from a trie
Or til a reid ourblawin with the wind.
Twa gods gyde me; the ane of tham is blind,
Ye, and a bairn brocht up in vanitie;
The nixt a wyf ingenrit of the se
And lichter nor a dauphin with her fin.
Unhappie is the man for evirmaire
That teils the sand and sawis the aire;
But twyse unhappier is he, I lairn,
That feidies in his hairt a mad desyre
And follows on a woman throw the fyre,
Led be a blind and teichit be a bairn.

The European dimension of the culture of the last Scottish court has been detailed by David Daiches in his book *Literature and Gentility in Scotland*. There he shows that the inspiration for the above poem came from a sonnet by Pierre de Ronsard which Alexander Montgomerie had already rendered into Scots. A strong French influence prevailed in Scotland long after the golden days of the Auld Alliance were curtailed by the Reformation. The contacts between French and Scottish literature were intimate and based on personal contact between the poets. Pierre de Ronsard had of course visited the Scottish court when he accompanied James V's first wife Madeleine de Valois to Edinburgh. Montgomerie was in the retinue of Esmé Stuart, Seigneur d'Aubigny, a Franco-Scottish aristocrat who became a favourite at the Court of James VI. The Court was thus a forcing house for European culture, but with Scots as its linguistic medium. The poets were encouraged in their art because they identified with each other as a group. Montgomerie begins a poem to an English poet at court, "My best belovit brother of the band" and the King himself addresses them as, "Ye sacred brethren of Castalian band". With the King's artistic enthusiasm and financial patronage, the writers regarded themselves and their poetry as important, indeed central to the life of the nation and her cultural identity. When James and his Court moved to London in 1603 both the patronage and the creative ambience disappeared, never to be replaced. From then on literature in Scots would explode sporadically on an increasingly anglicised scene because of the genius and commitment of individual writers, rather than a group of them. A centre for Scottish artistic life no longer existed. Another result was that the range of Scots literature narrowed. The court poets had exploited the full canon of the language, from the earthy and colloquial to the refined and aureate. With their departure the upper register of Scots all but disappeared – the top end of the market, so to speak – and Scots became more and more associated with the couthy, and the country rather than the courtly. Up till then poets had found within Scots everything they wanted to express, but with the departure of the Court they would now turn to English for their more refined utterances.

A few of the Castalian Band, poets such as William Fowler and Robert Ayton, actually accompanied James on his journey South, adopted English and became tolerable Cavalier poets. Ayton literally left Scots behind as he crossed the Tweed, describing it as,

> Faire famous flood which some tyme did devyde
> But now conjoyns two Diadems in one.

In a political sense the poet was right – Scotland and England were now the glittering diadems in James's crown, but in a linguistic sense the two parts of his realm would remain divided for a long time to come. Indeed, as I shall show later, the bridge over the Tweed which joins Coldstream and Cornhill also separates quite different linguistic communities. The spoken languages there remain to a great extent Scots in the north and English on the south of the river.

In literature, the high ground, so to speak, was given over to English. The poetry joined the elevated tones of the King James version of the Bible as a twin pillar of the prestige of the English language in a Scots-speaking country in the 17th century. Not only new poetry was written in English but works previously in Scots were anglicised increasingly. An edition of the King's collected works was printed in 1616. It has lost totally the original flavour of the writing. The fashion for things English was taking root at the top. Most expressions of regret for the old language would come much later when the belief that it was dying had firmly established itself. But there is one poem, in English by a Protestant Scot called Zachary Boyd (1583-1653), which has a fey wistful quality of nostalgia for a lost past, and criticism for those who follow fashion to the detriment of the native culture. I feel it sums up perfectly the linguistic duality which now prevailed in Scotland.

> Words fine before, are banished from the court
> And get no roome but with the countrey sorte;
> Men's mouthes like trees beare words as leaves that fall
> Now greene and good, anon are withered all.
> The words which whilom all men did admire
> Loath's in a trice may henceforth not appear,
> No more than changing French with gallant shews
> Could be content to weare the irish trewes;
> Our wordes like clothes, such is vain man's condition,
> In length of time does all weare out of fashion.
> We are like echo which by voice begot
> From hollow vales speakes wordes it knoweth not.

## Chapter 5

## The Confusion of Union

> It is true that the nations are *unius labii*, and have not the first
> curse of disunion, which was confusion of tongues, whereby
> one understood not the other. But yet, the dialect is differing,
> and it remaineth a mark of distinction. But for that, *tempori
> permittendum*, it is to be left to time. For considering that
> both languages do concur in the principal office and duty of a
> language, which is to make a man's self understood, for the rest
> it is rather to be accounted (as was said) a diversity of dialect
> than of language: and as I said in my first writing it is like to
> bring forth the enriching of one language, by compounding and
> taking in the proper and significant words of either tongue,
> rather than a continuance of two languages.

Francis Bacon's eloquent appraisal of the relationship between
the languages of the two Kingdoms, written the year after
James's accession to the English throne, is very much a vision
of an ideal Union. There, not one people or their language
is to predominate over the other; instead, their joint culture
will be a creative fusion of the best both has to offer. It never
happened. Instead, we begin to witness the attempt first by the
upper classes in Scotland and much later by the middle classes
to divest themselves of all trace of their native tongue. It was
to take them a very long time and was certainly unsuccessful
as far as speech was concerned until large numbers of wealthy
Scots began sending their sons to be educated at English public
schools towards the end of the 18th century. In the early 17th
century however the élite of the Scottish aristocracy were just
beginning to recognise London as the centre of their orbit. It
probably came as a great shock to them that language they
considered refined was regarded as comic by their peers at
court and in high society. In a way, the English reaction was
quite natural. Over two centuries later Lord Cockburn recalled
how an English accent was so strange to the boys of the Royal
High School that the arrival of an English pupil sent them into

paroxysms of laughter, whenever the unfortunate boy opened his mouth. The English lad was probably cut to the quick by their cruelty, and the Scots aristocrats in London probably felt much the same. However London was where the action was, and if to get a piece of it you had to swallow your pride and adapt to the manners of the Southern Metropolis, well . . . that would be home from now on. To mak the future siccar, many a Scot on the make invested in an English wife . . . gin faither wes a bittie coorse, weel at least the bairns wad hae the bon ton!

Typical of the attitude of the self-styled Scoto-Brittanes who formed James's retinue was that expressed by William Alexander, Earl of Stirling, in an introduction to his poetry published in 1603:

> The language of this Poeme is (as thou seest) mixt of the English and Scottish Dialects; which perhaps may be unpleasant and irksome to some readers of both nations. But I hope the gentle and Judicious Englishe reader will beare with me, if I retaine some badge of mine owne countrie, by using sometimes words that are peculiar thereunto, especiallie when I finde them propre, and significant. And as for my owne countrymen, they may not justly finde fault with me, if for the more parte I use the English phrase, as worthie to be preferred before oure owne for the elegance and perfection thereof. Yea I am perswaded that both countrie-men will take in good part the mixture of their Dialects, the rather for that the bountiful providence of God doth invite them both to a straiter union and conjunction as well in language, as in other respects.

Inevitably the content of the mix in writing was increasingly weighted in favour of the English option. Printing as we have seen was adapting to English models as early as the 16th century, and by the 17th the process was almost complete, with the old Scots spelling conventions rarely used. In manuscripts, however, the process of anglicisation was more gradual. Keith Williamson has described the change in the 17th and early 18th centuries as " . . . a shift from a fairly full Scots through an anglicised Scots to a Scotticised English." Much of the writing concentrated on the continued religious dispute that racked Scotland and is written in lofty biblical English. Other works, particularly the diaries that have come down to us, are in a more colloquial style, often following the writing conventions of the Scots of the previous century. John Nicoll was a Writer to the Signet who recorded events in Edinburh in the middle years of the century. Here he describes the Law's reaction to the falset [falsehood] and cheating endemic in God's Kingdom on earth: " . . . thair wes daylie hanging, skurging, nailling of luggis, and binding of pepill to the Trone, and booring of tounges; so that it was ane fatall yeir for fals notaris and witnessis."

Whether as a result of religious and political tension or the dilemma of finding a balance between the two languages, Scottish literature probably reaches its lowest ebb in the 17th century. By the 18th century, writers appear to have found a workable, at times brilliant, fusion of the two, and the best poetry of Ramsay, Fergusson and Burns is the result. But in the 17th century, the creative mix appears to have been beyond the Covenanter and Royalist poets who attempted it. The most successful poetry was very English, as is that of Drummond of Hawthornden, a friend and host to Ben Jonson, or very Scots in the case of Robert Sempill of Beltrees. Sempill's famous poem is a mock elegy on the Piper from Kilbarchan called Habbie Simpson. It is worth quoting from as it illusrates both the subject matter and the verse form that featured even more prominently in the following century. This poem was in fact extremely popular and widely known, so much so that the verse form in which it is written became known as Standard Habbie.

> Aye whan he play'd the lasses leugh
> To see him teethless, auld and teugh,
> He wan his pipes besides Barcleugh,
> Withouten dread!
> Which after wan him gear eneugh;
> But now he's dead.
>
> Aye whan he play'd the gaitlings gethert
> And when he spak the carl blethert
> On Sabbath days his cap was fethert,
> A seemly weid;
> In the kirk-yeard his mare stood tethert
> Where he lies deid.

The homely and parochial found ready expression in Scots, while the "high ground" of art poetry was almost entirely given over to English. But if the courtly tradition in Scots died a death, there was considerable compensation in the rise of a great folk literature and its expression in the ballads of the

Borders and the North-East. They occupy a subtle middle ground between the high and the low, the universal and the parochial, the aristocratic and the peasant. The language of the ballads appears to take the best from both English and Scots. Ballad Scots "may be said to include English and go beyond it" as Hamish Henderson describes it. The ballads of the Border lands especially are a curious mell of directness of speech and action yet fey other worldlinesss in ambience. The end of 'Tam Lin' where the Queen of Faerie addresses Janet illustrates the style perfectly:

> Out then spak the Queen o Fairies,
> And an angry woman was she:
> 'Shame betide her ill-far'd face,
> And an ill death may she die,
> For she's taen awa the boniest knight
> In a' my companie.
> 'But had I kend, Tam Lin,' she says,
> 'What now this night I see,
> I wad hae taen out thy twa grey een,
> And put in twa een o tree'

The ballads of course evolved in the oral tradition, crafted over many retellings. We shall never know if there was one original hand at work on any of them, or whether they emerged communally from cultural exchange by minstrels who wandered the land, bringing news and entertaining the people. What is perhaps apposite is that in the period which initiated the grave doubts many Scots entertain regarding their native culture, the country's finest literary creations were anonymous.

Linguistic anonymity, or the desire to conceal one's Scottishness by speaking like the English, did not reach bandwagon proportions until the following century, but its roots are already established in the 17th century. An English visitor to Scotland in 1689, the Reverend Thomas Morer, suggests that the upper classes would have to try harder, but the will was there:

> They have an unhappy tone, which the gentry and nobles cannot overcome, tho' educated in our schools . . . so that we may discover a Scotchman as soon as we hear him speak: Yet to say truth, our Northern and remote English have the same imperfection.

There are also signs however that there still existed a strong lobby among the same upper class which was proud of its speech. The following diarist admits to the provincial lack in his writing and his desire to purge it of Scotticisms, but he appears to be reasonably content with the way he speaks.

> You know I came to England the last time upon no other account, but to learn the language, and promised to keep correspondence with you upon this condition, that you would make remarks upon my letters, and faithfully Admonish me of all the Scoticisms, or all the words, and Phrases that are not current English therein. I confess I have a great Veneration for our own and the Northern English Language, upon the account of the Anglo-Saxon, to which they are so nearly ally'd; but yet . . . am as ambitious to write modern English, as any Gascon, or Provencal can be to write the modern French.

The feeling of inferior provinciality vis à vis the culture of England in general, and its writing and speech in particular also took a stronger and stronger hold on the élite, whose aspirations whether political or financial made them look to London. This is a comparatively new phenomenon. Before the Unions of the Crowns and of the Parliaments, Scots compared and contrasted their culture with others from the standpoint of independence. Their scope for self-criticism was international and, in the traditional ties with mainland Europe, healthily wide-ranging. Following the Unions, English culture came to dominate over all others, the only model for artistic and social life. The upper classes and later on the rising middle classes defined themselves not in a Scottish context but in an Anglo-British one. In this context, the thriving independent culture of the 15th and 16th centuries was forgotten and Scotland was regarded as a provincial backwater, rather like East Anglia or Yorkshire. Many individual Scots would continue to assert cultural independence and refuse to style themselves North Britons, but in many ways they were resisting both current fashion and the general way Scottish society was moving. Scotland could be regarded as both nation and region, the definition as today influenced by personal political and cultural aspirations.

In the 17th century, however, there were still many who thought Scottish culture had an important and equal role to play in the creation of a shared British culture. Alexander Hume, Rector of Edinburgh High School, belonged, like Bacon, to the school which thought English could benefit from an infusion of Scots. He addressed himself to the problem of devising a grammar for the language of the United Kingdom and tried to interest James VI in the project. Most of the pamphlet entitled *Of the Orthographie and Congruitie of the Britain Tongue* published around 1618 is pretty heavy going, but the following passage is of a livelier nature, treating as it does an argument about the nature of the mixture of the two dialects. Interestingly, he begins by criticising Scottish printers who are abandoning Scots for English conventions, even though the Scots spelling, he feels, more accurately reflects the spoken idiom.

> To clere this point, and alsoe to reform an errour bred in the south, and now usurped by our ignorant printeres, I wil tel quhat befel myself quhen I was in the south with a special gud frende of myne. Ther rease, upon sum accident, quhither quho, quhen, quhat, etc. sould be symbolised with a q or w, a hoat disputation betuene him and me. After manie conflictes (for we ofte encountered), we met be chance, in the citie of Baeth, with a Doctour of divinitie of both our acquentance. He invited us to denner. At table my antagonist, to bring the question on foot amang his awn condisciples, began that I was becum an heretik, and the doctour spering how, ansuered that I denyed quho to be spelled with a w, but with qu. Be quhat reason? quod the Doctour. Here, I beginning to lay my grundes of labial, dental, and guttural soundes and symboles, he snapped me on this hand and he on that, that the doctour had mikle a doe to win me room for a syllogisme. Then (said I) a labial letter cannot symboliz a guttural syllab. But w is a labial letter, quho a guttural sound. And therfoer w can not symboliz quho, nor noe syllab of that nature. Here the doctour staying them again (for al barked at ones), the proposition, said he, I understand; the assumption is Scottish, and the conclusion false. Quherat al laughed, as if I had been dryven from al replye, and I fretted to see a frivolouse jest go for a solid ansuer.

Thus has many a sound Scottish argument been shouted down by force of English numbers since the time of Union. Interestingly the pronunciation he refers to, the hw or chw sound we have in e.g. the word whales is still marked in Scottish speech. Even those Scots who speak what linguists call R.P. (Received

Pronunciation) and others 'Queen's, Oxford, or B.B.C."
English will still pronounce Wales and whales differently, unlike
the R.P. speakers in England. Hume's pamphlet is also a good
illustration of the mixed dialect at work in prose – his style is
still recognisably Scots. As the century wore on, though, and
the contact and mocking increased, the style becomes less
mixed and more English. The balance of the United Kingdom
was such that it was the Scots who had to travel to the English
capital and impress there. The English had no need or desire
to come North and impress the Scots in Scotland – no earthly
reason to adapt to their culture. The Scots were the minority
in the majority culture, and so it was assumed with the usual
arrogance of the larger partner in any union, that the minority
should eradicate its differences to accommodate the majority.

Another of the dissenting voices raised in defence
of the native tradition, was that of Sir George MacKenzie of
Rosehaugh, founder of the Advocate's Library and author of
numerous works on ethics and Scots law. In 1673 he wrote an
impassioned plea for Scots, directed at the English and included
in a preface to his book on legal rhetoric entitled *Pleadings*.
Note the change in the style that half a century has wrought
– unlike Hume, there is little specifically Scots in the writing
itself. It does however reveal the feelings of an upper-class Scot
of the late 17th century at the same time proud and defensive
about his native culture.

> It may seem a paradox to others, but to me it appears undeniable,
> that the Scottish idiom of the British tongue is more fit for
> pleading than either the English idiom or the French tongue;
> for certainly a pleader must use a brisk, smart, and quick way
> of speaking; whereas the English, who are a grave nation, use
> a too slow and grave pronunciation, and the French a too soft
> and effeminate one. And therefore, I think the English is fit
> for haranguing, the French for complimenting, and the Scots
> for pleading.
>
> Our pronunciation is like ourselves, fiery, abrupt, sprightly,
> and bold; their greatest wits being employed at Court, have
> indeed enriched very much their language as to conversation;
> but all ours bending themselves to study the law, the chief
> science in repute with us, hath much smoothed our language
> as to pleading: And when I compare our law with the law of
> England, I perceive that our law favours more pleading than
> theirs does; for their statutes and decisions are so full and

authoritative, that scarce any case admits pleading, but (like a hare killed in the seat) 'tis immediately surprised by a decision of statute. Nor can I enough admire why some of the wanton English undervalue so much our idiom, since that of our gentry differs little from theirs; nor do our commons speak so rudely as those of Yorkshire. As to the words wherein the difference lies, ours are for the most part old French words, borrowed during the old league betwixt our nations, as cannel for cinnamon, and servit for napkin, and a thousand of the like stamp; and if the French tongue be at least the equal of the English, I see not why ours should be worse than it. Sometimes also our fiery temper has made us, for haste, express several words into one, as "stour" for dust in motion; "sturdy" for an extraordinary giddiness, &c. But generally words *significant ex instituto;* and therefore one word is hardly better than an other: their language is invented by courtiers, and may be softer, but ours by learned men and men of business, and so must be more massy and significant; and for our pronunciation, besides what I said formerly of its being more fitted to the complexion of our people than the English accent is, I cannot but remember them, that the Scots are thought the nation under heaven who do with most ease learn to pronounce best the French, Spanish and other foreign languages, and all nations acknowledge that they speak the Latin with the most intelligible accent; for which no other reason can be given, but that our accent is natural and has nothing, at least little, in it that is peculiar. I say not this to asperse the English, they are a nation I honour, but to reprove the petulancy and malice of some amongst them who think they do their country good service when they reproach ours.

We must also remember that underlying much of the Englishman's hostility to the Scots in those days was jealousy aroused by the invasion of his capital by thousands of Caledonians decidedly on the make. Both at court in the 17th century and at Parliament in the 18th century they had tremendous political influence, which they tried to keep to themselves.

The relationship between Dr Johnson and his biographer James Boswell reveals much about the tension between Scots and English identities in London society. In an exaggerated form their relationship sums up the relative status and attitudes abroad at the time regarding culture in general and language in particular. Boswell is a typical 18th-century upper-class Scot doing everything he can to ingratiate himself with the London literati and nobility. Dr Johnson is a good example of the élitist Englishman, resentful of the Scots' inordinate influence in every sphere of city life and disdainful of their culture and their attempts to acquire his. Boswell's description of their first meeting encapsulates the ambience abroad in the English capital.

> Mr Davies mentioned my name, and respectfully introduced me to him. I was much agitated; and recollecting his prejudice against the Scotch, of which I had heard much, I said to Davies, "Don't tell him where I come from." – "From Scotland," cried Davies roguishly. "Mr Johnson," said I, "I do indeed come from Scotland, but I cannot help it." I am willing to flatter myself that I meant this as a light pleasantry to soothe and conciliate him, and not as an humiliating abasement at the expense of my country. But however that might be, this speech was somewhat unlucky; for he seized the expression "come from Scotland," which I used in the sense of being of that country; and retorted, "That, Sir, I find, is what a very great many of your countrymen cannot help." This stroke stunned me a good deal; and when we had sat down, I felt myself not a little embarrassed, and apprehensive of what might come next.

What came next was that Boswell got the name of being Johnson's "Scotch cur", becoming – and here I must beg forgiveness of the gracious reader for the impropriety of introducing a Scotticism – the classic sook. The liaison had its reward nevertheless, in the finest biography in the English language. Boswell was prepared to suffer all insults and indignities in order to record the great man's sayings. His near family did not share his enthusiasm. His father Lord Auchinleck, like many of the law lords, continued speaking Scots, which he used to good effect when he heard of his son's attachment to Johnson: "Jamie has gaen clean gyte . . . whae's tail dae ye think he has preened himsel tae noo? A dominie man! – an auld dominie, wha keepit a schule an caaed it an Acaademy!" Johnson's manners during his tour of Scotland apparently justified the animal imagery frequently attributed in descriptions of him. Boswell's wife was so put out at the sight of her husband grovelling before the Englishman, she remonstrated that she "had often seen a bear lead by a man, but never till now had she seen a man lead by a bear!" An indication of the good Doctor's insensitivity and his supercilious dismissal of the notion that the Scots possessed any degree of culture at all are revealed by his remarks, made in obvious wonder and admiration when he visits an innovative school for the handicapped in Edinburgh:

> It was pleasing to see one of the most desperate of human calamities capable of so much help: whatever enlarges hope will exalt courage; after having seen the deaf taught arithmetick, who would be afraid to cultivate the Hebrides?

Boswell of course was so thirled to Johnson, and like many Scots of the age so in thrall to English culture that he was all but oblivious to the great lexicographer's faults. He was particularly sensitive about his Scottish accent and frequently rails against the speech of his fellow countrymen when he comes across then in London: "the common style of company and conversation, the coarse jibes of this 'hamely' company . . . the Fife tongue and the Niddry's Wynd address were quite hideous." Contemplating that he may have to go back and live in Scotland in order to inherit his estate fills him with horror; "like yoking a Newmarket winner to a dung cart." Given his linguistic insecurity, any praise or hint of approval from his master fell like manna from heaven, and is therefore worthy of note in his Diary. The following passage is from 1772:

> On Saturday, March 17, I introduced to him Sir Alexander Macdonald. Sir Alexander observed, "I have been correcting several Scotch accents in my friend Boswell. I doubt, Sir, if any Scotchman ever attains to a perfect English pronunciation."

> JOHNSON. "Why, Sir, few of them do, because they do not persevere after acquiring a certain degree in it."

> Upon another occasion I talked to him on this subject, having myself taken some pains to improve my pronunciation, by the aid of the late Mr. Love, of Drury Lane theatre, when he was a player at Edinburgh, and also of old Mr. Sheridan. Johnson said to me, "Sir, your pronunciation is not offensive." With this concession I was pretty well satisfied; and let me give my countrymen of North Britain an advice not to aim at absolute perfection in this respect. A small intermixture of provincial peculiarities may, perhaps, have an agreeable effect.

The great literary language of the makars, two centuries on, regarded as a provincial peculiarity! This was how far Scots had sunk in the second half of the 18th century. It was to sink even farther, and be regarded with odium by men who did not share Boswell's undiscriminating veneration for the English. David Hume was one of many Scots who felt no personal affinity with the English. He felt at home only in Edinburgh or Paris where he was fêted by the intelligentsia, and was for ever railing against "the factious barbarians of London, who will hate me because I am a Scotsman and am not a Whig, and despise me because I am a man of letters". This did not prevent him following blindly the fashion of the age for Augustan refinement, the attainment of which necessitated the rooting out of all trace of Scottishness from one's writing and if possible, one's speech.

With first the aristocracy then the upper and middle classes adopting English manners there began the slow percolation down through the social ranks of English models of speech. Scots in literary use was deemed appropriate only when dealing with the speech of the lower orders. As we have seen, this process was taking place throughout the century following the Union of the Crowns. But the social downgrading of Scots continued at a more rapid and unchecked pace following the Union of the Parliaments in 1707, when the anglicising tendencies reached obsessive proportions among the upper echelons of society.

The balancing act which the Scots of the 18th century made between Scottish and English culture in their society and within the individual, produced an almost schizophrenic state of mind among people whose loyalties were constantly pulled in different directions. Allan Ramsay the painter, helped found the Select Society in 1754. From its ranks sprang the Society for the English Language whose initial aim was to promote the correct use of English, and to that effect engaged a Mr Leigh, "a person well qualified to teach the pronunciation of the English tongue with propriety and grace".

Whereas in the previous century the terms to describe the language of the Lowlands alternated between English and Scots, as it had done interchangeably since the 16th century, there was now a conscious distinction made between the vernaculars of England and Scotland. As late as the first few decades of the 18th century, when schools referred to subjects available on their curriculum they would describe the class teaching the vernacular as the Scots class or the English class, and the terms would not imply a difference of emphasis in language teaching. By the middle of the 18th century, however, schools began to refer to teaching English "by the new method", which usually implied that an attempt would be made to teach southern pronunciation. Heriot's school in the 17th century claims it will "teach the bairns to reach and write Scots distinctly", while by the time Edinburgh Academy is founded in the early 19th century, "a proper English articulation and accent" is insisted upon "in order to remedy a defect in the education of boys in Edinburgh who are suffered to neglect the cultivation of their native tongue and literature during the whole time they attend the grammar schools". As you can see, by then English has become so all-powerful that it is deemed "proper" and the "native tongue" while presumably the indigenous vernacular, the actual native tongue is dismissed as a defect! We are now beginning to recognise traits engraining themselves which persist in our own similarly Enlightened Age.

The modern fallacy of Scots as a corruption of English really took root in the later 18th century. In order to facilitate the well-nigh impossible acquisition of spoken English, numerous books were published in Scotland which attempted to show by multifarious orthographic devices, how English was pronounced in England. Today, English orthography is a minefield for students from foreign countries, where the same symbol can represent totally different sounds e.g. gh in tough and through. If you do not know how they should be pronounced you will get little help from the orthography and are therefore prone to making mistakes in your pronunciation. The Scots were in the same position in the 18th century. Having little or no contact with native English speakers on a regular basis, their position was rendered even more difficult because they did not realise that many of the sounds they made were in fact Scots and not English. Among the books published for the help of our forefathers in this their hour of need were: *The Edinburgh New Method of Teaching English* by Godskirk and Hume in 1750, *Linguae Brittanicae Vera Pronunciato* by James Buchanan in 1757, *The Pronouncing Dictionary of the English Language* by John Burns in 1777, and William Scott's *A General View of English Pronunciation* published in Edinburgh in 1784.

The last attempts systematically to give numbers to the various vowel sounds in English and by breaking up the words into numbered segments, reveal how they should be pronouced. He also points out common Scottish confusions: "bliss (made a verb) for bless, rid for red: o short with o long, as lo-ng for long and most for mo-st." The differentiation of the English sounds in not and note, clock and cloak or cot and coat was particularly confusing for Scots speakers, and they frequently got it, and still get it wrong. While dubbing the commentary, in English, for the television programmes called 'The Mother Tongue' I used the verb forge pronouncing it with the same sound as door or bore. My unwitting Scottisicm was immediately seized upon, and I was assured that the correct pronunciation of forge was to rhyme it with gorge or George. However, knowing where such concessions landed our ancestors, I stuck to what came naturally to me and pronounced the word as always, "foarge". I use the example to illustrate the survival of Scots in our English pronunciation and also to show how difficult it must have been for the anglicisers. One of the results of the confusion was that many Scots overcompensated, and put imagined English pronunciation to words where Scots and English shared the same sound e.g. if box is pronounced boax in Scots but box in English, it follows that coach in Scots must be coch in English and pork pronounced poark in Scots must needs be pawrk in English. The latter sound is still to be heard among "polite" speakers in Edinburgh today. The effect of this mixter-maxter must have been gey hilarious at times, as our ancestors frequently pit their fuit in it. The 20th-century dramatist, Robert McLellan, portrayed the problem beautifully in his play *The Flouers o Edinburgh,* set in the period in question in an Auld Reikie awash with anglicisation. In this short scene a Scottish Augustan poet, Mr Dowie, is just being disabused of the notion that he writes English with propriety, by young Charles who has returned from London speaking a strangulated bourach of a pronunciation he insists is London English:

> CHARLES: Here we are, I think. Yes. You are sitting among the skulls Doctor, addressing Death. You say:
> They boney hand lies chill upon my breast.
> Now add my carcase to they loathsome feast.
> DOWIE: Breist, no breast.
> CHARLES: I know it has to read breist before it rhymes, but an Englishman says breast.
> DOWIE: B-R-E-A-S-T?

CHARLES: Yes
DOWIE: Breist
CHARLES: No, breast
DOWIE: An Englishman says breast, for b-r-e-a-s-t?
CHARLES: Yes, Doctor, have you ever been to England?
DOWIE: Na.
CHARLES: I thought so. English as a spoken language is quite foreign to you.
DOWIE: But I read naething else.
CHARLES: I said as a spoken language. You cannot possibly know how English words should sound. You have no right to write English poetry.
DOWIE: Nae richt! Dae they say that in London?
CHARLES: Englishmen say that.
DOWIE:Dear me. A lot o my rhymes are wrang, then?
CHARLES: A considerable number.
DOWIE: Dear me.

Dowie is racked to the core of his existence by this revelation, but his type persisted and went to even greater lengths to acquire bon ton. In the Scottish capital in particular a roaring trade for those practising the new science of elocution was available. In the 1760s a horde of out-of-work actors and linguistic eccentrics flocked to Edinburgh to teach English. Among their pupils were men who in their saner moments were outstanding philosophers, scientists and economists – the brilliant coterie of Enlightenment intellectuals who made Edinburgh one of the cultural capitals of Europe at the time. David Hume was so embarrassed with what he considered to be his inability to speak or write perfect English, that when he died he is said to have confessed, not his sins, but his Scotticisms! With Hume it appeared to be an idée fixe to out-English the English. He is said to have sent his manuscripts to such diverse experts as a linen-draper in Bristol and a cobbler in Norwich, in order to have any trace of Scotticism weeded out of the text before exposing it to the scrutiny of polite society. This from a man who was proudly Scottish and whose sceptical view of religion enraged large sections of that society, and who retained his principles till his dying day. Hume and his group were susceptible, gullible prey for the teachers who set up shop to give courses throughout the long Edinburgh winters. Advertisements like the following appeared in the newspapers, placed by teachers such as William Noble intent on exploiting upper class sensibilities:

THE CONFUSION OF UNION

> . . .taking all imaginable care of the quantity, accent and
> manner of expression, by which he hopes that the barbarisms,
> so often and so justly complained of here, will be properly
> guarded against.

That one is taken from the *Caledonian Mercury* of 19 September
1761. Ten years later in the *Edinburgh Evening Courant* a Mr
Telfer, "lately arrived from London" offers classes which will
not only promote English but make sure that no other language
rears its head.

> Having studied and taught the English language chiefly for
> several years past, he hopes he shall be able to teach his pupils
> that pronunciation and accent which are used by the most
> polite speakers and great care will be taken that no Scotch be
> spoken in time of school.

Mr Telfer stresses that he has spent some time in London to
recommend himself to his charges. As most of the audience
hadn't the faintest idea of what London English actually
sounded like, scope for gulling private pupils must have been
enormous. A London accent, far from being required, was
actually quite a rarity among the teachers. Two of the most
successful were Masson, an Aberdonian, and Sheridan, a
Dubliner. The mind boggles as to what kind of English their
pupils came out with. Boswell attended Sheridan's course of
lectures, and the *Scots Magazine* reports that he was in the
company of 300 gentlemen "the most eminent in this country
for their rank and abilities". Those few teachers who were
native speakers of the required dialect of course could score
points against those who had learned the right accent. In the
preface to his highly successful *Only Sure Guide to the English
Tongue; or New Pronouncing Spelling book of 1776,* one of
the English teachers, William Perry, berates "North British
authors like Masson, the late Mr Drummond, etc; some of
whom probably never crossed the Tweed." Mr Perry undertook
a series of lectures in Edinburgh. His advertisement in the
*Caledonian Mercury* shows how entertainment and music hall
mixed with the serious attempt to teach refinement in speech.
Presumably to illustrate the opposite of what he is aiming at
and to introduce some burlesque black humour, he promises
in the course of his lecture to introduce " . . . the following

89

characters, viz The Schoolboy, Schoolmaster, Common Reader, Monotonist, Jingler, Stammerer, Word-monger, Clipper, Coiner and Distorter . . . " One of the elocutionists actually advertised his lecture as "a new species of literary entertainment" and Edinburgh was that hoatching wi language teachers, one gets the feeling that many were simply jumping on a bandwagon, exploiting a fashion which in fact did not last much longer than a decade. Perry was obviously an expert in public relations. In order to cheer up and encourage his audience, he reveals to them that even in England there are pockets of language practise more uncouth than Scots' " . . . specimens of the dialects of several counties of England remarkable for their barbarism and corruption of speech." Perry and the rest of the teachers probably realised that there was little hope of changing the ladies and gentlemen who attended their lectures. They were set in their ways, their ways were Scots and it would be a few generations yet before that would alter. But if you caught them young enough, the children's ways could be set on a different course. A pointer of things to come is indicated in a report of Mr Perry's visit to a class in Leith in the *Caledonian Mercury* of 6 May 1776.

> What is very remarkable is that the youngest class, some of whom are not four years of age, repeated the different sounds of the vowels and diphthongs from Mr Perry's New Pronouncing Spelling Book to an astonishing degree of accuracy.

Another facet of the rush to acquire English was the publication of articles and books which gave detailed lists of "Scotticisms liable to be mistaken for English in this country". The first collection was compiled by James Elphinstone and was published, not surprisingly, as an appendix to Hume's *Political Discourses* in 1752. Elphinstone also published a supplementary list in the *Scots Magazine* in 1764. One of the areas he highlights is the the problem of Scots stressing words on different syllables from the English. Our countrymen, " . . . so remote from propriety and unaided by system" naturally got things wrong; they stress e.g. April and harrass on the last syllable, ally and perverse on the penultimate syllable, clandestine and contribute on the antepenultimate syllable. When you have worked that lot out, you soon discover that many of these features which were excruciatingly embarrassing to the 18th century cognoscenti have since become accepted pukka R.P. English! James Beattie, the poet, and compiler of one of the best-selling volumes, stressed in his introduction that he wanted his readers to beware of using expressions which seemed English, but are in fact the remnant of that huge area where Scots and English shared the same vocabulary but expressed it in different ways. One can only smile today when one thinks of men of the stature of David Hume and Adam Smith being fashed with trivialities such as the following examples from the book:

| SCOTS | ENGLISH |
|---|---|
| a bit bread | a bit of bread |
| the better of a sleep | the better for a sleep |
| a sore head | a headache |
| to my bed | to bed |
| he has got the cold | he has got a cold |
| where do you stay | where do you lodge, live, or dwell? |

A glance at the two lists will show that the Scottish options are still in use in Scottish English today, proof of the survival of Scots even among those who don't consider they speak it. The anglicisers were perhaps more successful in the long term with the words that were unique to Scots. Beattie never regarded them as much of a problem:

> With respect to broad Scotch words, I do not think any caution requisite, as they are easily known and the necessity of avoiding them is obvious.

The tragedy is that the Scots no longer took what they wanted from other cultures to enrich their own, as had been the case in the days of the makars. They adopted uncritically English fashion and taste not realising that their attempt to write in the style of Addison, Pope or Shenstone was doomed to the same kind of failure as the attempt to root out their native idiom from their speech. In his autobiography which spans the years from 1722 to 1805, Dr Alexander Carlyle of Inveresk relates how he had been taught "a tolerable accent" of English by his aunt from London, "an accomplishment which in those days was very rare". His journal details the life of the Scottish community in London, in particular their frequenting of the

British Coffee House, the London Scots' favourite rendezvous. English was desired by the Scots, but for many it remained an impenetrable, foreign jargon. In one incident in 1758, Carlyle asks a fellow Scot, Dr Charles Congalton, what he thinks of the English now that he has been among them for a few months? He replies that he is unable to reply honestly as he has not really made acquaintance with any of them, " . . . I never enter into conversation with the John Bulls, for, to tell you the truth, I don't yet well understand what they say." Carlyle knew personally many of the leading men of the Enlightenment such as William Robertson, Principle of Edinburgh University, whom he recalled, " . . . spoke broad Scotch in point of pronunciation and accent or tone . . . his was the language of literature and taste, and of an enlightened and liberal mind." The great geologist James Hutton, Sir Walter Scott, and many others continued speaking Scots as their natural language long after the fashion for Augustan elegance had abated.

In writing, however, prose had become almost completely unscotched by the latter half of the 18th century. Yet it had not yet become English. When Lord Mansfield commented to Alexander Carlyle his feeling that he was not reading English in the works of Hume and Robertson, the sage of Inveresk gave this perceptive reply:

> to every man bred in Scotland the English language was in some respects a foreign tongue, the precise value and force of whose phrases he did not understand and therefore was continually endeavouring to word his expressions by additional epithets or circumlocutions which made his writing appear both stiff and redundant.

The Scots literati had as yet mastered only the surface level of English, a detached register devoid of emotional resonance. They wrote English perfectly and with propriety, in the same way as for example a German intellectual who had similarly become fluent in the language and mastered its structure and surface would have done. Ironically this foreignness of English written by Scots, with its painstaking, precise correctness and formality, made it the perfect medium for discussing science and philosophy in whose various branches the men of the Scottish Enlightenment excelled.

# Chapter 6

## The Vernacular Revived?

For work requiring both head and heart, in creative literature, this surface grasp of the English language that the Scots writer had was all but useless. The Scots literati of course were so in thrall to English taste at the time that they never realised how forgettable their attempts to copy Augustan English in fact were. Indeed, they were blind to literary brilliance on their own doorstep. Henry MacKenzie's important review of Burns' Kilmarnock edition in the prestigious periodical *The Lounger* is favourable up to a point, but the fashion for English propriety and elegance gets in the way of objective criticism:

> One bar indeed, his birth and education have opposed to his fame, the language in which most of his poems are written.

Fortunately, Burns was enough of his own man to ignore the advice of the literary élite to write solely in English; otherwise he would have been just another obscure stilted versifier, like Blacklock or Beattie, instead of one of the world's genuinely popular yet great poets. All the Scots writers however engaged in a balancing act between the two cultures . . . but it was only when the poets Allan Ramsay, Robert Fergusson, and Burns wrote in Scots that the balance tilted from precious gentility towards greatness – proof, if any is required, that Scots still held the heart if not the mind of the intelligentsia of the period.

For running throughout the 18th century with its obsession to anglicise there arose the parallel cultural phenomenon of pride in Scots and the vigorous continuation of its tradition as both a medium for literature and speech. The motivation behind this was diverse and often surprising, taking in notions of national and religious identity; reaction against artificial gentility; the desire to prove that with a sprinkling of Scots a poet need not desert propriety; academic promotion of the Scottish past as a source of pride in Scottishness at a time when that identity was under threat; and the simple conclusion that, in Scots, Scottish people could communicate more effectively and writers write more relevantly of the Scottish experience. Many of these strands can be traced in the work of the poet who is very much the father figure of the Vernacular Revival, Allan Ramsay. In the Preface to *The Ever Green*, his collection of Scots poetry from before 1600, he upbraids his fellow writers for their present predilection for setting their works in the classical landscapes of Europe, instead of rooting them, like the makars, in their native environment. In the ancient poetry, he claims:

> The Morning rises (in the Poet's description) as she does in the Scottish Horizon. We are not carried to Greece or Italy for a Shade, a Stream or a Breeze. The Groves rise in our own Valleys; the rivers flow from our own Fountains, and the Winds blow upon our own Hills. I find not Fault with those Things, as they are in Greece or Italy: But with a Northern Poet for fetching his Materials from these places, in a Poem, of which his own Country is the Scene; as our Hymners to the Spring and Makers of Pastorals frequently do.

You will notice that the style of the Preface is not uninfluenced by the sententious neo-classic tones of his English contemporaries; indeed a quotation from Pope, is printed on the title page of *The Ever Green*. The Preface also goes on to rail against those Scots so thirled to present fashion that they hardly admit to knowledge of their native tongue. This is an early example of the rise of the "Kent his faither" syndrome which bedevils many Scots' views on their native culture and its exponents.

> There is nothing can be heard more silly than one's expressing his Ignorance of his native Language; yet such there are, who can vaunt of acquiring a tolerable Perfection in the French or Italian Tongue, if they have been a Forthnight in Paris or a Month in Rome: But shew them the most elegant Thoughts in a Scots Dress, they as disdainfully as stupidly condemn it as barbarous. But the true Reason is obvious: Every one that is born never so little superior to the Vulgar, would fain distinguish themselves from them by some Manner or other, and such, it would appear, cannot arrive at a better Method. But this affected

Class of fops give no Uneasiness, not being numerous; for the most part of our Gentlemen, who are generally Masters of the most useful and politest Languages, can take Pleasure (for a Change) to speak and read their own.

Ramsay here describes a provincial cast of mind in the culturally colonised minority of fops who automatically dismiss their native culture out of hand; these were unfortunately to increase in number over the next two hundred years as members of the Establishment and their many imitators gave themselves over almost entirely to English culture. But there was also an important group who, while absorbing English culture, also found time and commitment for the native tradition and patriotically fostered this alternative cultural world picture. In Edinburgh, for example, the Episcopalian and Jacobite coterie was a powerful cultural and political force. Ramsay's *Ever Green* was printed by Thomas Ruddiman, an Episcopalian Jacobite activist and propogandist from the North-East. He printed the Jacobite newspaper, the *Caledonian Mercury* and brought out editions of Gavin Douglas and the Latin poet George Buchanan. All of these efforts were tied in with a deliberate attempt to propogate the pre-Reformation humanist tradition in Scottish letters and provide a viable alternative to the Presbyterian version of Scottish culture. Ruddiman's printing of *The Ever Green* and Ramsay's interest in Scotland's literary past were almost certainly inspired by a product of the other major printing press in Edinburgh in the first quarter of the 18th century. James Watson was also a staunch Jacobite, and his *Choice Collection of Comic and Serious Scots Poems both ancient and modern* (1706-1711) fulfilled a popular demand for knowledge of the glories of the past, especially in the form which has never really ceased to be popular, that of Scots song. Hamilton of Bangour and Hamilton of Gilbertfield are two of a large group of minor writers who wrote in Scots and contributed songs and poems to the various collections published at this time. Bangour was a romantic charmer who composed poems to seduce the belles of the city. He was out in the '45 Rebellion and was forced to leave his homeland for exile in France after Culloden. His most popular work was the ballad "The Braes of Yarrow". The Jacobites apparently combined politics and pleasure in equal measure, their clubs like the Horn, the Auld Stuarts, and The White Cockade meeting in the steeran howffs o Auld Reekie where songs like "Awa Whigs Awa" or "The Wee Wee German Lairdie" were chorused, and the toast, in claret, was "The King ower the Water". Ramsay's friend, Wiliam Hamilton of Gilbertfield, celebrated the non-political activities of the coterie.

> The dull-draff drink maks me sae dowff
> A' I can do's but bark and yowff;
> Yet set me in a claret howff
> Wi' folk that's chancy,
> My muse may len me then a gowff
> To clear my fancy.
>
> Then Bacchus-like I'd bawl and bluster
> And a' the muses 'bout me muster
> Sae merrily I'd squeeze the cluster
> And drink the grape
> 'T wad gie my verse a brighter lustre,
> And better shape.

> (*dull-draff drink* thin ale; *dowff* weary; *bark and yowff* rant and rave; *gowff* slap)

Hamilton of Gilbertfield also revived Blin Hary's *Wallace*, translating it curiously into English. It was this version however that kindled a fervent patriotism in young Robert Burns. From the Covenanting west country, Burns was neither Episcopalian, nor Jacobite but he shared the same love of Scotland and its culture with his great literary predecessors of the 18th century, Allan Ramsay and Robert Fergusson. Like Fergusson, who also belonged to the Episcopalian group, Burns carried on the interest in Scots song shown by the earlier poets, devoting the last years of his life to their collection and reworking. But the undoubted commitment and brilliance of the three greatest of the poets was not enough to stem the slow erosion of Scots in life and letters. Lacking the support of the establishment, the survival of the Scots tradition now depended on individuals going against their socialisation and saving Scots from the imminent death the establishment wished on the language and to a lesser extent its literature. This has been the case from Ramsay through to MacDiarmid.

While the use of Scots was narrowed to reflect the speech of the lower orders, this also had the effect of giving the language a radical irreverent quality which it has retained ever since. The writers could adopt the persona of the common man and criticise and satirise society with impunity. When Burns acknowledged his debt to the individual who had gone before him, Robert Fergusson, he also took a swipe at the condescension of the upper classes:

> My curse upon your whunstane hearts
> Ye Enbrugh gentry!
> The tythe o' what ye waste at cartes
> Wad stow'd his pantry!

The different social status of Scots and English determined the kind of poems written in the two registers. In English, Burns tends to look over his shoulder to see the reaction of his aristocratic patrons and polite society. In Scots, he attacks with vigorous directness all the ills in his society, from a local quack doctor in 'Death and Doctor Hornbrook' to the Kirk satire of 'The Holy Fair' and the swingeing portrait of the failings of an individual Calvinist in 'Holy Willie's Prayer'.

> O Thou that in the Heaven dost dwell,
> Wha, as it pleases best Thysel,
> Sends ane to heaven an' ten to Hell
> A' for thy glory,
> And no for onie guid or ill
> The've done before thee!

The Calvinist belief in the Elect, or chosen few who will go to heaven, is perfectly expressed in that verse. Burns goes on to describe the earthly imperfections of those who see themselves as the Elect, using humour to bring home the point.

> Yet I am here, a chosen sample,
> To show thy grace is great and ample:
> I'm here a pillar o' Thy temple,
> Strong as a rock,
> A guide, a buckler and example
> To a' Thy flock!

> But yet, O Lord! confess I must:
> At times I'm fash'd wi' fleshly lust;
> An' sometimes, too, in warldly trust
> Vile self gets in;

But Thou remembers we are dust,
Defiled wi' sin.

O Lord! yestreen, Thou kens, wi' Meg –
Thy pardon I sincerely beg –
O, may't ne'er be a living plague
To my dishonour!
An' I'll ne'er lift a lawless leg
Again upon her.

Besides, I farther maun avow –
Wi' Leezie's lass, three times, I trow –
But, Lord, that Friday I was fou,
When I cam near her,
Or else, Thou kens, Thy servant true
Wad never steer her.

Despite these "minor" transgressions, Willie feels confident enough in his status as one of the chosen, to demand that the Lord bring the full weight of his awesome fury down upon a "major" transgressor called Aitken of Ayr Presbytery, who has dared ridicule the Auld Licht conservative party that Willie belongs to in the Kirk. Having done his vengeful duty by the Elect, Willie exhorts the Lord to return to his normal role, that of looking after Willie and his kind:

But Lord, remember me and mine
Wi' mercies temporal and divine,
That I for grace an' gear may shine
Excell'd by nane;
And a' the glory shall be Thine –
Amen, Amen!

Burns focuses on the woes of the country and the village, a parochial setting which his poetry, like that of all great artists transcends and renders universal. The man he called his elder brother in the Muse, Robert Fergusson, died tragically young, before his 25th birthday. But he left us a gutsy realistic description of Scottish urban life in the middle of the 18th century. While others such as Ramsay in *The Gentle Shepherd* indulged in the fashion for pastoral poetry, a vogue for rusticity perfectly suited to the image of Scots as a peasant dialect, it is refreshing to come across Fergusson's starkly naturalistic portrayal of the darker side of street life in the capital city. This passage from 'Hallow-Fair' describes police violence by the

City Gaurd, a corps made up, as you can guess from the poet's transcription of their speech, of Gaelic-speaking Highlanders who had little love for their Lowland countrymen:

> Jock Bell gaed furth to play his freaks,
> Great cause he had to rue it,
> For frae a stark Lochaber aix
> He gat a clamihewit
> Fu' sair that night.
>
> 'Ohon!' (quo' he), 'I'd rather be
> By sword or bagnet stickit,
> Than hae my crown or body wi'
> Sic deadly weapons nicket.'
> Wi' that he gat anither straik
> Mair weighty than before,
> That gar'd his feckless body aik,
> An' spew the reikin gore,
> Fu' red that night.
>
> He pechin on the causey lay,
> O' kicks and cuffs weel sair'd;
> A Highland aith the serjeant gae,
> 'She maun pe see our guard'.
> Out spak the weirlike corporal,
> 'Pring in ta drunken sot.'
> They trail'd him ben, an' by my saul,
> He paid his drunken groat,
> For that neist day.
>
> Guid folk, as ye come frae the fair,
> Bide yont frae this black squad;
> There's nae sic savages elsewhere
> Allow'd to wear cockade.
> Than the strong lion's hungry maw,
> Or tusk o' Russian bear,
> Frae their wanruly fellin paw
> Mair cause ye hae to fear
> You death that day.
>
> (*clamihewit* blow; *straik* blow; *weirlike* warlike; *groat* small coin; *wanruly* unruly)

The seemier side of city life is also an area which Allan Ramsay excells in portraying. He deliberately goes out of his way to shock genteel society with poems of low-life characters such as the bawd, Lucky Spence:

My bennison come on good doers,
Who spend their cash on bawds and whores;
May they ne'er want the wale of cures
      For a sair snout
Foul fa' the quacks wha that fire smoors,
      And puts nae out.

My malison light ilka day
On them that drink and dinna pay,
But tak' a snack and run away;
      May't be their hap
Never to want a gonorrhea,
      Or rotten clap.

(*wale* choice; *snout* protuberance; *smoors* damps downs: *snack* bite, short time)

Yet the same Ramsay and his Jacobite patriots read the *Spectator* at every meeting of their gentlemen's club, The Easy Club, in order to perfect their English, so that

by a Mutual improvement in Conversation they may become more adapted for fellowship with the politer part of mankind.

Success for the poet wigmaker's efforts to write with propriety came in his enormously popular pastoral play *The Gentle Shepherd*. It received the ultimate stamp of approval when Pope expressed himself to be delighted by it, when his friend Dr Arbuthnott read and translated it for him at his grotto in Twickenham. This was doubly pleasing for Ramsay, because in the play there is a wide range of linguistic styles reflecting in an idealised way the linguistic identity of the varying classes in Scottish society. It was proof to a patriot, that fashion could still be adhered to without deserting Scots.

Burns similarly indulged in both sides of his dual inheritance. At times it is as if he needs to balance Augustan purity with down-to-earth Scots bawdry. In his letters and prose however, Burns the Augustan is very much to the fore. The Dedication which prefaces his Edinburgh edition of 1787, is addressed to the Noblemen and Gentlemen of the Caledonian Hunt. It is typical of the high rhetorical style fashionable then:

My Lords and Gentlemen, – A Scottish Bard, proud of the name, and whose highest ambition is to sing in his Country's service – where shall he so properly look for patronage as to the illustrious Names of his native Land; those who bear the honours and inherit the virtues of their Ancestors? The Poetic Genius of my Country found me as the prophetic bard Elijah did Elisha – at the plough, and threw her inspiring mantle over me. She bade me sing the loves, the joys, the rural scenes and rural pleasures of my natal Soil, in my native tongue: I tuned my wild, artless notes, as she inspired. She whispered to me to come to this ancient metropolis of Caledonia, and lay my songs under your honoured protection: I now obey her dictates.

The only extended prose which Burns wrote in Scots is the tour de force of a letter he sent to his friend William Nicol in Edinburgh, from Carlisle towards the end of his Border tour. In it we get an idea of the colloquial spoken Scots Burns was familiar with in his south-west part of the country. We also have a virtuoso performance by a man taking gleeful delight in words and their possibilities. In fack it's that stowed an thrang wi fouth o guid Scots words wi nae English equivalent, ye'll hae tae owreset it yersels. I wad be faur ower forjesket e'en tae begin!

Carlisle 1st June 1787—-or
I believe the 39th o' May rather

Kind, honest-hearted Willie,

I'm sitten down here, after seven and forty miles ridin, e'en as forjesket and forniaw'd as a forfoughten cock, to gie you some notion o' my landlowper-like stravaguin sin the sorrowfu' hour that I sheuk hands and parted wi' auld Reekie. – My auld, ga'd Gleyde o' a meere has huchyall'd up hill and down brae, in Scotland and England, as teugh and birnie as a vera devil wi' me. – It's true, she's as poor's a Sang-maker and as hard's a kirk, and tipper-taipers when she taks the gate first like a Lady's gentlewoman in a minuwae, or a hen on a het girdle, but she's a yauld, poutherie Girran for a' that; and has a stomach like Willie Stalker's meere that wad hae digeested tumbler-wheels, for she'll whip me aff her five stimparts o' the best aits at a down-sittin and ne'er fash her thumb. – When ance her ringbanes and spavies, her crucks and cramps, are fairly soupl'd, she beets to, and ay the hindmost hour the tightest. – I could wager her price to a thretty pennies that, for twa or three wooks ridin at fifty mile a day, the deil-sticket a five gallopers acqueesh Clyde and Whithorn could cast saut in her tail. –

I hae dander'd owre a' the kintra frae Dumbar to Selcraig, and hae forgather'd wi' monie a guid fallow, and monie a weel-far'd hizzie. – I met wi' twa dink quines in particlar, ane o' them a sonsie, fine fodgel lass, baith braw and bonie; the tither was a clean-shankit, straught, tight, weel-far'd winch, as blythe's a lintwhite on a flowerie thorn, and as sweet and modest's a new blawn plumrose in a hazle shaw. – they were baith bred to mainners by the beuk, and onie ane o' them has as muckle smeddum and rumblegumtion as the half o' some Presbytries that you and I baith ken. – They play'd me sik a deevil o' a shavie that I daur say if my harigals were turn'd out, ye wad see twa nicks i' the heart o' me like the mark o' a kail-whittle in a castock. –

I was gaun to write you a lang pystle, but, Gude forgie me, I gat myself sae noutouriously bitchify'd the day after kail-time that I can hardly stoiter but and ben. –

My best respecks to the guidwife and a' our common friens, especiall Mr & Mrs Cruikshank and the honest Guidman o' Jock's Lodge. –

I'll be in Dumfries the morn gif the beast be to the fore and the branks bide hale. –

> Gude be wi' you, Willie! Amen ——
>
> ROBt BURNS

Interestingly, while many of his nobler contemporaries spoke Scots and wrote English, Burns appears to have been at home speaking both Scots and English, a forerunner of the truly bilingual society that Lowland Scotland was to become. Many of the literati who met him during his Edinburgh period testified to his refined command of English, and one commented that David Hume was far broader in speech than the Ayrshire ploughman. To paraphrase another great Ayrshire writer of our own day, William McIlvanney, Burns and the other poets of the vernacular revival "inhabited the paradoxes" of their cultural milieu, as writers like McIlvanney are still doing successfully today. The dichotomy in Scottish society, in other words did not produce a clean divide between a pro-Scots and pro-English faction in matters of language, culture and politics; the divide existed within individuals who were now heir to both the Scots and the imported English tradition. For some the choice of calling oneself Scottish or North British was an arbitrary one, for others the assertion of a Scottish identity under threat was of paramount importance. That divide, I would maintain, still exists within the Scottish psyche today.

The Scots of the 18th and 19th century revivalists was a mixed dialect of the two languages, reflecting more the prestige of English rather than any great change to the everyday speech of the mass of the population. The way they wrote their Scots also reflects the English ascendency. With little knowledge of the old ways of spelling, apostrophes are used in abundance to suggest the English letter that is missing e.g. gie becomes gi'e, o become o', an becomes an'. This gives the impression that Scots is derived from English, and in those days of ignorance about how languages evolve, this became the accepted myth. In other words, Scots came to be seen as a debased dialect of English, rather than the dialect remnants of what was once the national language of Stewart Scotland.

The mixed dialect however also gave writers a wonderfully flexible medium. Rhymes are a lot easier to master where you have two words, or two pronunciations to chose from. In 'Tam o' Shanter' for example, Burns uses Scots one minute, English the next, in order to get the second half of his rhyming couplets to match. Some lines, such as the following, require the English pronunciation for the rhyme to work:

> Gatherin her brows like gathering storm,
> Nursing her wrath to keep it warm

Ayrshire Scots pronounces the o in storm like the o in Scottish Standard English (SSE) quorum. This obviously does not rhyme with warm in its English form, and even less so in its Ayrshire Scots form, where warm is pronounced like the SSE word farm. Other rhymes require one word to be pronounced in English, the other in Scots for the rhyme to work. The Ayrshire Scots for a well, for example, is pronounced wal, with the a pronounced like the SSE a in Balham. In order to make the word rhyme with the Scots "hersel" however Burns choses the English form well,

> And near the thorn, aboon the well
> Whare Mungo's mither hang'd hersel

And of course there are many examples where both rhymes are Scots, and knowledge of the Scots pronunciation is required to make the rhyme true. For example floods and woods do not rhyme in English, but in Burns and my own Kyle dialect the vowel sound in both words is somewhat like that in SSE bid, and so the rhyme works for the Scots speaker, though it does not work in English.

> Before him Doon pours all his floods,
> The doubling storm roars thro' the woods

In the hands of a master like Burns, the two languages fuse imperceptibly into a perfect whole, an extension of the potential of both registers. To paraphrase what was said earlier about the language of the Border ballads, Burns' Scots contains English yet goes beyond it, while his English includes Scots and goes beyond it as well. From this fertile fusion emerged many of his greatest lyrics. Burns also proved that this language could express the philosophic concerns of the age as well as Augustan English. But the Scots does it in a more tangible and direct fashion, as these verses at the beginning and end of 'To a Mouse' surely demonstrate.

> Wee, sleeket, cowran, tim'rous beastie,
> O, what a panic's in thy breastie!
> Thou need na start awa sae hasty
> Wi' bickering brattle!
> I wad be laith to rin an' chase thee,
> Wi' murdering pattle!
>
> I'm truly sorry man's dominion
> Has broken Nature's social union,
> An' justifies that ill opinion
> Which makes thee startle
> At me, thy poor, earth-born companion
> An' fellow mortal! . . . . . . ..
>
> That wee-bit heap o' leaves an' stibble,
> Has cost thee monie a wearie nibble!
> Now thou's turned out, for a' thy trouble,
> But house or hald,
> To thole the winter's sleety dribble,
> An' cranreuch cauld!
>
> But Mousie, thou art no thy lane,
> In proving foresight may be vain:
> The best-laid schemes o' Mice an' men
> Gang aft agley,
> An' lea'e us nocht but grief an' pain,
> For promis'd joy!

Still thou art blest, compar'd wi' me!
The present only toucheth thee:
But och! I backward cast my e'e,
On prospects drear!
An' forward, tho' I canna see,
I guess an' fear!

(*brattle* sudden rush; *cranreuch* frost; *agley* awry)

This Scots was also the language of the songs he collected
or wrote and whose popularity he established all over the
world. 'Auld Lang Syne' has versions I'm sure in a hundred
languages, most of which are more agreeable to Scots lugs
than the Anglo-American adaptation 'Old long Zyne'! His love
songs, such as 'Ae Fond Kiss', or 'Flow Gently Sweet Afton',
again are popular in the English-speaking world for this very
reason; they can be read as Scots or English, though to Scots
speakers they have an extra dimension which knowledge of his
native language brings to all his work. Of all the love songs he
wrote, there is none greater than his anthem to international
brotherhood in which he again reconciles his native Scots
with Augustan English terms, to produce a memorable mell
of the two:

Then let us pray that come it may
(As come it will for a' that)
That Sense and Worth o'er a' the earth
Shall bear the gree an' a' that!
For a' that, an' a' that,
It's comin yet for a' that,
That man to man the world o'er
Shall brithers be for a' that.

(*bear the gree* win supremacy)

The brilliance of Burns' achievement, and the genuine
popularity of his work and that of Fergusson and Ramsay
before him did have some effect in the way Scottish society
viewed the language. One of the most curious effects is still
with us today, for I came across it often when I travelled the
country to make the television series "The Mother Tongue"
for B.B.C. Scotland. J. Derrick McClure in a brilliant essay in
*Chapman* magazine identifies it as the Pinkerton Syndrome,
after an 18th-century Scottish historian, John Pinkerton, who

stated the following in a preface to a collection called *Ancient Scottish Poems, never before in print* published in the same year as the Kilmarnock Edition, 1786.

> . . . none can more sincerely wish a total extinction of the Scottish *colloquial* dialect than I do, for there are few *modern* scoticisms which are not barbarisms. . . Yet I believe, no man of either kingdom would wish an extinction of the Scotish dialect in poetry

In a country which is justifiably proud of a literature which stems directly from the life of its people, this desire to separate the living dialect from the literary medium is a dangerous one in its inevitable consequences; Scots is forced into a ghetto where it is only used for poetry and it is denied status in any other sphere. The contemporary equivalent of the Pinkerton Syndrome is a belief among teachers that they are fostering Scots by teaching their wards to perform one or two party piece poems in the language, usually for public performance at Parents' Night, yet the language is banned as a respected medium of communication inside the classroom 99% of the time the children spend there. In other words it is all right for a wee divertissement, but the last thing you want to do is encourage and extend what after all is a "corrupt dialect"! Pinkerton's language is archaic, but the belief and the message has emerged from many a schoolmaster's lips in the two intervening centuries:

> An heroic or tragic tale, in the pure Buchan dialect, would be very acceptable. But beware the common fault of taking cant phrases for old speech. Use the words of the vulgar, but use ancient and grave idioms and manner. Remember this vulgar speech was once the speech of heroes.

McClure gets to the nub of the Scots and English tension within individuals of then, and tragically now, and his conclusion makes a point which is both incisive and depressing for those of us who value the continuation of a Scottish tradition independent of that of England.

> The Pinkerton Syndrome is a mode of defence against this uncomfortable fact: an attempt to retain traces of a Scottish identity without disturbing the 'British' status quo. The study of the things that once gave Scotland its distinctive national

character but are now safely consigned to the past is permissible or even meritorious: the study of the things that now give it this, and if recognised and cultivated could do so to a much greater extent, is taboo.

McClure's thesis fits many of the Scots literati of the 18th century. Some, such as James Thomson and Thomas Campbell, unscotched themselves completely in their writing. Further, they achieved fame by composing those great hymns of British or pan-English Nationalism, 'Rule Britannia' and 'Ye Mariners of England'. Perhaps even these two committed Anglophiles felt pangs of unease on hearing the verse of 'God Save the King' which crows about the crushing of "rebellious Scots", and sought to establish their song as the new National Anthem? But other arch-Anglicisers such as Beattie and astonishingly, Boswell reveal their desire to retain some Scots as a badge of identity. Beattie personifies the Pinkerton syndrome perfectly, for while publishing lists of Scotticisms to be avoided he still found time to write the occasional verse in Scots himself. The opening of his poem To Mr. Alexander Ross, an important North-East poet, reveals exactly the parameters of his interest in the language – the past and the peasantry!

> O Ross, thou wale of hearty cocks,
> Sae crouse and canty with thy jokes!
> Thy hamely auldwarl' muse provokes
> Me for awhile
> To ape our guid plain countra' folks
> In verse and stile.

In his journal for 1763 Boswell refers to a fellow Scot in London, Alexander Wedderburne, who had also attended Sheridan's English classes in Edinburgh two years before. His conclusion will be a surprise to many who presume he wanted no trace of his native land to be obvious in his speech.

> . . . and though it was too late in life for a Caledonian to acquire the genuine English cadence, yet so successful were Mr. Wedderburne's instructors, and his own unabating endeavours, that he got rid of the coarse part of his Scotch accent, retaining only as much of the "native wood-note wild," as to mark his country; which, if any Scotchman should affect to forget, I should heartily despise him.

On a completely different plane from the Genteel Anglicisers, were a large and kenspeckle group of people who continued using Scots, often to spite those going in the opposite direction. The great law lords of the 18th and early 19th centuries, for example, were famous for their pithy use of Scots. The law was probably the most important and prestigious profession open to the scions of the aristocracy in Scotland after the Union. It is significant that its practitioners continued its tradition of linguistic as well as its institutional independence from England. One anecdote concerning John Clerk of Penicuik, later Lord Eldin, relates how the Scot was arguing a Scottish appeal case before the House of Lords. Pleading his client's use of a burn by prescriptive right, Clerk's rich Scots rang out referring to ". . . the watter haein rin that wei for mair nor forty year" The Chancellor, bemused by Clerk's pronunciation interrupted his oration and inquired in a rather condescending tone: "Mr. Clerk, do you spell water in Scotland with two t's?" Clerk, astonished by the man's rudeness, still managed to give better than he got. "Na, na, my lord" he replied, "We dinna spell watter wi twa t's, but we spell mainners wi twa n's!"

For some of the judges their use of Scots was a reaction against the fashion for precious gentility particularly prevalent in Edinburgh during the fashion for the cult of Sensibility, when grown men would weep in public at sentimental, sententious works such as Henry MacKenzie's *The Man of Feeling*. The sensibility of such as the hanging judge, Lord Braxfield was of a quite different order. During the deplorable sedition trials at the turn of the 19th century, the Englishman Margarot claimed that he and his fellow radicals stood in a long line of noble men who were reformers as well – Jesus Christ himself being one of them. "Muckle he made o that", Braxfield replied, "He was hangit!" Lord Kames' farewell address to the Court of Session when he retired from that august institution in his eighties is memorably concise and terse: "Fare-ye-aa weel, ye bitches"

The other belief which emerged towards the end of the 18th century and has been repeated ever since is that Scots is dying. In some ways this has been a benevolent myth, for when something is on the point of extinction, preservation societies spring up to defend it. This was true elsewhere in a Europe dominated by the ideas of the Romantic Movement with it's vogue for ancient "peasant" civilisations and threatened traditional ways of life. Burns and later James Hogg were accepted by the literati as they fitted into the fashionable stereotype of the untutored genius rising out of the "Volk" or people. Walter Scott's novels with their brilliant use of Scots in dialogue sold all over the world, and he and Burns enjoyed tremendous vogue in translation, especially in Germany and France. The despised dialect was simultaneously the language of the "natural genius" European civilisation craved, possibly as an escape from the Industrial Revolution which was destroying the old order.

History was re-interpreted to suit the latest fashion. Henry MacKenzie, who had criticised Burns' use of Scots a few generations before, could look back from the vantage point of old age, conveniently forget about his previous disdain for Scots and write:

> There was a pure classical Scots spoken by genteel people, which I thought very agreeable; it had nothing of the coarseness of the vulgar patois of the lower orders of the people.

Safely in the past, Scots could now be remembered nostalgically by those à la recherche du temps perdu. As we shall see, in the 19th century, Scots and Romanticism gae haund in haund, and not only among the peasantry. The literati would now recall old aunts and dowager duchesses who spoke vivid Scots, while in their youth they would have disowned them for shame, or certainly would never have boasted either the fact of them speaking Scots, or being fond personal acquaintances and relatives. For despite all the pressures against the language, the thrawn auld raucle tongue still came naturally to most Scots most of the time, at the turn of the 19th century. The working class spoke nothing else, the upper class was now admitting that they had spoken it until very recently (yestreen) and the only section which now stood as a bulwark against the "barbaric dialect" was the expanding middle class, who again would have spoken Scots against their better wishes. Their feelings about the language are expressed by their champions, the ministers, who from Unst in the North to the Solway in the South compiled that amazing document of Scottish social history, *The Statistical Account* of the late 1790s. The Account is chock full of references to local speech, and almost all are unfavourable. The wishful thinking behind the statement of the Minister of Peterhead is typical. It depicts the ignorance and extreme naivety of his class on the subject of language and its nature.

> The language spoken in this parish is the broad Buchan dialect of the English, with many Scotticisms, and stands much in need of reformation, which it is hoped will soon happen, from the frequent resort of polite people to the town in summer.

Some hope!!

# Chapter 7

## The Last Scotch Age?

Two very different patriots from the Scottish upper classes, Sir Walter Scott and Lord Cockburn, were torn between love for Scottish culture and the feeling that the future lay with ever closer ties to England. Scott was very much a Tory who revelled in the feudal past, Cockburn a committed Whig whose drafting of the Scottish Reform Bill in 1832 did much to create a more democratic Scotland. Cockburn was convinced the 18th century had been ". . . the last purely Scotch age. Most of what had gone before had been turbulent and political. All that has come after has been English." Yet neither really made a committed and sustained stand against the erosion of specifically Scottish institutions such as the law or education which was going on in their lifetime. The deep dilemma of their compromised Scottish patriotism is illustrated by an incident described in Lockhart's *Life of Scott*. Following a debate about reforming the Court of Session on English lines, Scott leaves the Faculty of Advocates with Jeffrey and some of his reforming friends:

> . . . who complimented him on the rhetorical powers he had been displaying, and would willingly have treated the subject-matter of the discussion playfully. But his feeling had been moved to an extent far beyond their apprehension: he exclaimed, 'No, no – 'tis no laughing matter; little by little, whatever your wishes may be, you will destroy and undermine, until nothing of what makes Scotland Scotland shall remain.' And so saying, he turned round to conceal his agitation – but not until Mr Jeffrey saw tears gushing down his cheek – resting his head until he recovered himself on the wall of the Mound. Seldom, if ever, in his more advanced age, did any feelings obtain such mastery.

Language figured prominently in both men's notion of Scottishness. Their contemporaries recall that both spoke broad Scots, and their writings are full of references to their pride in Scots, a pride tinged with their belief that the language is changing. The same Scottish patriotic feeling was behind the publication of Jamieson's *An Etymological Dictionary of the Scottish Language* in 1808, and the founding of publishing clubs such as the Maitland and Bannatyne, which sought to encourage interest in Scotland's past history and literature. The Scots language was regarded by the type of Scotsman behind these ventures as a national asset under threat. Lockhart recalls Scott's reverence for his aunt who had spoken "her native language pure and undiluted, but without the slightest tincture of that vulgarity which now seems almost unavoidable in the oral use of a dialect so long banished from Courts." In his *Journal* of 11 August 1844 Lord Cockburn wrote:

> English has made no encroachment on me; yet, though I speak more Scotch than English throughout the day, and read Burns aloud, and recommend him, I cannot get even my own children to do more than pick up a queer word of him here and there. Scotch has ceased to be the vernacular language of the upper classes.

What Cockburn does not go on to say is that the reason his sons have little Scots, is that he has sent them to the Edinburgh Academy, the first school in Scotland to model itself on the English public schools, where Scots was banned and the English of England fostered. Both Scott and Cockburn were founders of the Academy, and presumably agreed with its language policy. Their love of Scotland and Scottish culture was romantic rather than practical and would not be allowed to hinder the progress of youth. In this aspect, loyalty to their class is more crucial than loyalty to their culture. For when the Scottish upper classes frequently state that Scots is dying, and revel in nostalgia for the generation before when all classes spoke Scots, they are distancing themselves from the fact that Scots was still spoken in an undiluted form by the vast majority of the population. Scott mentions a classical Court Scots which survived until recently in the older generation of aristocrats, a language quite different from the vulgar patois of his own day. The language had not really changed, it was simply that with the upper classes having deserted it, what was considered fine before was now deemed vulgar. When Dean Ramsay wrote his *Reminiscencies of Scottish Life and Character* in 1857, he was anxious to stress of the older generation of ladies such as Miss Erskine of Dun, that while speaking "downright Scotch. Every tone and every syllable was Scotch. . . .Many people now would not understand her. She was always *the lady* notwithstanding her dialect, and to none could the epithet vulgar be less appropriately applied". Dean Ramsay's book has many examples of Scots as spoken by these daughters of the aristocracy, some of them are very amusing; Lady Perth, for example said to a Frenchman who was boasting of the superiority of the French cuisine compared to the Scottish, "Weel, weel, some fowk like parritch, and some like puddocks." Interestingly a hundred years after the Miss Erskine of Dun referred to by Ramsay had disappeared from the face of the earth, and by implication the Scots language of her class, there appeared the brilliant Scots writing of another Miss Kennedy Erskine of Dun, Violet Jacob. Her work is perfect testimony to the fact that there are exceptions to every rule in something ultimately as personal as language. Her sensitivity to Scots proves that at least some daughters of the aristocracy were not entirely assimilated into English ways.

While the tiny aristocratic and industrial élite of the 19th century attempted to educate their children in England or at English schools in Scotland, the mass of working-class and probably middle-class people continued hearing and speaking only Scots. For it was not until after the Scottish Education Act of 1872 that any systematic attempt was made to teach spoken English in Scottish schools. From then on Inspectors were able to institutionalise and enforce attitudes already entrenched in society. Even then, the changes would take a long time to percolate through the system, and actually permanently affect the speech of the pupils. State inspection was initiated in Scotland as early as 1845, but very few were employed in that role. One of the earliest inspectors, J. Kerr, wrote a volume of reminiscencies of his early days in the job. This is how he recorded a teacher in the North-East describing his practice in teaching reading:

> Weel, I begin them wi' wee penny bookies; but it's no lang till they can mak' something o' the Testament; and when they can do that, I chuse easy bits oot o' baith the Auld and New Testaments that teaches us our duty to God and man. I dinna say that it's maybe the best lesson book; but it's a book they a'

hae, and ane they should a' read, whether they hae ither books
or no. . . and when I see them gettin' tired o' their lessons and
beginning to tak a look about the house, I bid them ..tak' their
pamphlets and story books. Ye ken, bairns maun like their books.

The same teacher, when reading from the Bible or other works
in English, would have adopted a very different register – the
English he would have heard all his life from the pulpit. He
would have tried to instruct his children to read in the same
register. But the language of everyday communication, indeed
the language of general instruction was still Scots. Until the
advance of English literature in Scottish universities in the
middle of the 19th century, Latin and the humanist tradition
had dominated Scottish higher education. Latin was the
language of learning, Scots the vernacular. Referring to Melvin,
the Rector of Aberdeen Grammar School in the 1850s, John
Hill Burton spoke of the man's "shyness of competing in the
language of England with Englishmen". A report from one of
the Inspectors in 1852 highlighted the fact that most teachers
in Lowland Scotland were influenced by

the Scotch dialects, to whom many of them have been accustomed
from infancy, and which are still used by the great majority
of those, with whom they have daily intercourse, and who, till
lately, derided the conversational use of English in one from
among themselves, calling him *Anglified* or *pedantic*.

As the century wore on and the Inspectors increased
in numbers and influence after the 1872 Education Act, the
attempt was made to insist that teachers and pupils should
communicate in a form of English. Up till then, literacy
in English had been the principal aim. If children could read
and write English, the teacher would feel he was doing his
job. Now English as a spoken language was to be actively
encouraged, and the children's Scots, presumably, actively
discouraged. This was the beginning of education appearing
as an alien imposition to many Scots, as their home language
was systematically devalued and banned from the school. The
Inspectors reports are full of references to the two-language split
of school and playground. Some realise that Scots should be
allowed in the junior classes to encourage the pupils, and act
as a bridge between their everyday language and the new one

they have to master in school. Some enlightened Inspectors, such as Mr Muir complained of the emphasis on artificially promoting English by rote learning. His report of 1876 recalled:

> In one school I asked a junior class the meaning of the word 'passenger' in the lesson before them. I was answered readily, 'one who travels by a public conveyance'. 'Quite right,' said I. 'Now what is a public conveyance? Give me an example. Tell me any public conveyance you have ever heard of?' There was a painful silence.
> Far preferable to this are the rough and ready explanations in colloquial, or even vernacular speech I sometimes get. Of a history class I asked one day the meaning of the word 'treason' What do you mean by committing treason against the king?' 'Gie'in him impudence,' was the prompt answer of one boy. 'Well, right so far, but tell me a little more accurately, what it is.' 'Speakin back to him.' It is obviously more pleasant to get such answers than answers like those which define 'invasion' as entering a country with hostile intentions.

Mr Muir's type were increasingly in a tiny minority as the anglicising momentum gathered pace and power. More and more, teachers and inspectors hearing children speak Scots would define it as 'giein impudence' to the teacher. With the schools relying on a satisfactory report from the Inspector to obtain their state grant, the uniformity insisted on by the Inspector in language had to be obeyed, even by those who disagreed with the policy, and regarded it as hindering rather than helping a child's articulacy and linguistic development. Literature in the children's native vernacular as well was regarded as inimical to the advance of English. From Inspector King's report of 1904, the Ballads were being taught all over the Border area at the turn of the century, but if they took heed of his report, the national literature as well as the language would be confined to what the bairns could pick up at home.

> Excellent as they are in themselves, and most appropriate to Border schools, the study of them should not absorb much of schooltime, although they might very well be learned at home in the winter evenings. The same criticism applies except to a limited extent to the introduction of poems by Burns and Hogg, and to all other writings however fine, which are not written in good modern English. This must be the staple of instruction, if we are to give the children the fullest possible equipment in

words and thought for modern life. The rest is luxury whatever the perfervid nationalist may say.

Many will recognise the contemporary ring to that statement, indeed it is so common for establishment figures in Scotland to be agents of cultural genocide, that what in fact is a barbaric negation of civilisation and culture is accepted blandly as the norm. Anyone who stands up for Scottish culture is automatically classed "a perfervid nationalist". With their home language and culture given no status whatsoever, and their literary and intellectual tradition increasingly ignored within education, it is little wonder that the Scottish identity is a confused blur at times. Perhaps the most astonishing phenomenon is the survival of the language and the identity it expresses, given the pressure to anglicise that runs through this "internally colonised" country of ours. For despite the anglicising momentum which got stronger as the century advanced, the 19th century was still a period of great achievement in Scots literature; Sir Walter Scott, James Hogg, and John Galt were novelists of major stature in the first half of the century, while Robert Louis Stevenson and George Douglas Brown gave the tradition a lift towards the century's close. In addition there were many less gifted writer such as Susan Ferrier, Mrs Oliphant and the group of "Kailyard" novelists, all of whom nevertheless contributed to an understanding of Scottish life in a period of great social change. In all of these writers, the use of Scots in dialogue gives the raciness and vigour of the speech of real people to their work. Contrasted with the anglified or English dialogue of the "nobler" characters, the novelists are able to exploit Scotland's wide range of linguistic styles to give texture and character to their novels. There is only enough room here to give two short examples. Here is Neil Blane, the landlord of the howff near Drumclog in Scott's *Old Mortality*, giving advice to his daughter on how to handle the Covenanters and Royalist soldiers in the pub.

> Aweel, take notice, Jenny, of that dour, stour-looking carle that sits by the cheek of the ingle, and turns his back on a' men. He looks like ane of the hill-folk, for I saw him start a wee when he saw the red-coats, and I jalouse he wad hae liked to hae ridden by, but his horse (it's a guid gelding) was ower sair travailed; he behoved to stop whether he wad or no.

Serve him cannily, Jenny, and with little din, and dinna bring the sodgers on him by speering ony questions at him; but let na him hae a room to himsell, they wad say we were hiding him. . . Aweel when the malt begins to get aboon the meal, they'll begin to speak about government in kirk and state, and then, Jenny, they are like to quarrel – let them be doing – anger's a drouthy passion, and the mair they dispute, the mair ale they'll drink; but ye were best serve them wi' a pint o' the sma' browst, it will heat them less, and they'll never ken the difference.

The next extract is from R.L. Stevenson's short story, *Thrawn Janet*, which is unusual in that it is entirely written in Scots, but as you can see, it is very much the spoken voice written down, rather than a deliberate attempt to sustain a Scots prose.

About the end o July there cam' a spell o' weather, the like o't never was in that countryside; it was lown an' het an' heartless; the herds couldnae win up the Black Hill, the bairns were ower weariet to play; an' yet it was gousty too, wi' claps o' het wund that rumm'led in the glens, and bits o' shouers that slockened naething. We aye thocht it but to thun'er on the morn; but the morn cam', an' the morn's morning, and it was aye the same uncanny weather, sair on folks and bestial. Of a' that were the waur nane suffered like Mr Soulis; he could neither sleep nor eat, he tauld his elders; an' when he wasnae writin' at his weary book, he wad be stravaguin' ower a' the countryside like a man possessed, when a'body else was blythe to keep caller ben the house.

Stevenson and the Kailyard writers tended to use Scots when dealing with themes set in the country or the small town. This reflected a narrowing of the range of the literature, and perhaps a refusal to cope with a rapidly changing Scotland where people flocked to overcrowded cities, and the industrial experience was more typical than the rural idyll depicted in the Kailyard. The literature became increasingly escapist, the universal in the works of Scott and Burns descending to the parochial in Ian Maclaren and S.R. Crockett. A couthy Scotland was depicted and lapped up by Scot and foreigner alike. Countries such as America had been raised on the novels of Walter Scott, so the Scots dialogue of the Kailyard writers presented no problems for them; besides, the popularity of Scots songs kept the language alive there as well. The 19th century was also a time in which thousands of Scots left home to create the empire and settle in every corner of the globe. They took their language with them, and all over the English-speaking world you will find poetry about Canada, Australia, New Zealand etc, written in Scots. A good example of the genre are the following verses from Charles Murray's poem 'Scotland Our Mither' written in South Africa at the turn of our own century.

> Scotland our Mither – this from your sons abroad,
> Leavin' tracks on virgin veld that never kent a road,
> Trekkin' on wi' weary feet, an' faces turned fae hame,
> But lovin' aye the auld wife across the seas the same.
>
> Scotland our Mither – we've bairns you've never seen –
> Wee things that turn them northwards when they kneel down at e'en;
> They plead in childish whispers the Lord on high will be
> A comfort to the auld wife – their granny o'er the sea.
>
> Scotland our Mither – since first we left your side,
> From Quilimane to Cape Town we've wandered far an' wide;
> Yet aye from mining camp an' town, from koppie an' karoo,
> Your sons richt kindly, auld wife, send hame their love to you.

At the end of the century, Scots and sentimentality went hand in hand. George Douglas Brown sought to "stick the Kailyard like pigs" with his vitriolic counterblast to the couthiness of small-town life in *The House with the Green Shutters*, but even he sees Scots only in terms of the fey and the other worldly. The Ayrshire of his time was full of miners and mill-workers who spoke a down-to-earth Scots, but Brown talks only of "the Kyle folk's. . . .graphic picturesqueness of speech". In an essay on John Galt's mastery of dialect he refers to the author's "habit of queer metaphorical expression". Brown hated the Kailyard, but he and Stevenson who both transcended it, were also influenced by it. Feyness, Scots, sentimentality and death are all contained in this scene from *Beside the Bonnie Brier Bush*, one of the classic Kailyard novels by Ian Maclaren. Here, George Howe, dying of tuberculosis, offers up a prayer for his unbelieving schoolmaster, Domsie.

> Lord Jesus, remember my dear maister, for he's been a kind freend to me and mony a puir laddie in Drumtochty. Bind up his sair heart and give him licht at eventide, and may the

maister and his scholars meet some mornin' where the schule never skails, in the Kingdom o' oor Father.

Stevenson too, despite using Scots to good effect also indulges in the death wish affecting people's views of the language and culture. Scots was all around him, yet he chose to write of it in this way in 'The Maker To Posterity'.

> Few spak it than, an' noo there's nane
> My puir auld sangs lie a' their lane,
> Their sense, that aince was braw an' plain,
> Tint a' thegither,
> Like runes upon a standin' stane
> Amang the heather.

The literature descended to the nostalgic and the provincial, and it would take a World War and a man called Hugh MacDiarmid to haul it back to a literature of national and international concern. Once again, the revival would be in Scots, still MacDiarmid's and most Scots' mither tongue. Educational reports apart, another strong indicator of the continuation of Scots as the everyday language of the people lies in the burgeoning popular press of the 19th century. William Donaldson has made an extensive study of Scottish newspapers in this period, and has been struck by the amount of Scots printed, both in reported speech, letters to the Editor and regular features by local characters. If the literature was getting nostalgic, the people could still write Scots as it was spoken; the language of the people, whose often radical world picture was expressed by it. This is "Maansie o' Slushigarth" giving an alternative view to the arrival of a new steamer service to Lerwick, which he says will only benefit the "jantry" or gentry.

> Diel hae me if da warld be na just gaen gyte! Da Lurick fock shuttin' wi' cannon, an' lightin' a der collies an' caandles an' dennerin' an' drinkin' an' rejoisin' aboot a fule ting o' a stemmer ship itt da Queen is sent ta carry da jantry's letters every ook ta da sooth! Fule moniments itt dey irr! What gude'ill dis stemmer shipp doe ta wiz puir fock? Will shoe mak meal ony shaper? Truggs! am fear'd shoe'll doe nae gude ava' 'cept helpin' wirr jantry ta gaing awa' ta da sooth wi' less spewin'. Na, na, I aye saiditt nae gude wid come o' new faingled tins an it'ill shune come to pass itt dis stemmer i'll mak kye an' sheep an' butter an' eggs an' a' kind o' kyuntry proddick muckle dearer. Forby da scores an' dizzens an' maybe hunders o' idle jaantin'

bodkies it'll be comin' frae da south just lek da locusts itt cam da Egypt davoorin da substance o' da laand! An de'll be tellin' wiz itt kens muckle betterit wi' shu'd hae rodds an' packets an' ferryboats an' inns, and muckle mair nonsense, just ta help dem ta rin o'er an' devoor wiz in a shorter time. Deil cut dem aff!

In the heart of the industrial central belt, an edition of the *Hamilton Advertiser* in 1889 contains this description of the town environment. There is an awareness also of the change in that environment, but no nostalgia.

There were thae gawsie, gash guidwives, wi' dirty faces and toozie heids, staunin' clatterin' wi' ane anither at every close mooth an' corner, while their weans were tumlin' ower ilk ither in the glaur, and their hooses at hame lyin' in confusion, as if some earthquake frae Sooth America had been gien' them a ca' in the byegaun'. Of coorse it's heartsome tae see sic an increase o' the population, and it's guid for the bakin business – but for my pairt, I wud prefer the bonnie green fields as they used tae be instead o' thae evidences o' the spread o' ceevilization.

The great social changes which took place in Scotland throughout the 19th century undoubtedly had an effect on the way people in different areas and different classes spoke. The muckle rich fermtouns of the eastern and north-eastern Lowlands had to a great extent replaced the small farmer with his croft. With their bothies and chalmers thrang with scores of ploughmen, the environment acted as a forcing house for traditional song and strengthened the status of the Scots of the area. When Gavin Greig and J.B. Duncan undertook the monumental task of collecting the folk tradition in the Buchan area at the turn of our own century, even they were probably astonished at the wealth of the material still sung – over 3000 songs. The Aberdeenshire songs are marvellously evocative of time and place. My own favourite is 'Mormond Braes', a song of lost love:

Oh there's juist as guid fish in the sea,
That's ever yet been taken,
I'll cast my net an try again,
For I'm only aince forsaken.

So fare-ye-weel ye Mormond Braes,
Where aft times I've been cheery,

Fare-ye-weel ye Mormond Braes,
For it's there I lost my dearie.

Oh there's mony's the horse has snappert an fa'n
An risen again fu early
There's mony's the lass has tint her lad
an gotten anither richt fairly.

If the country areas remained strong in their Scots, it was very much because the way of life was maintained despite the changes in the size of the farms – it was very much the same people who inhabited the crofts and the fermtouns. In the industrial cities, social change also resulted in a huge influx of thousands of outsiders into areas which had traditionally been Scots-speaking. Gaelic or English-speaking Highlanders and Irish, English and Scots-speaking people from Ulster, especially Donegal, were the two main groups of incomers, but the melting pot was stirred by the addition of Italian, Yiddish, and Lithuanian-speaking immigrants. What emerged from all this was a lingua franca which had lost some of the distinctive features of the local Scots dialect in order to accommodate the multifarious group of people who now communicated in it. It still remained Scots, for the immigrants adapted the language they came into contact with, and among the workers, that was not Oxford English. Many words we think of as belonging to the Scots of Glasgow, are derived from the native tongues of the main immigrant communities; the derogatory term for a Glaswegian, keelie is from the Scots Gaelic *gille*, a boy, while the Irish word *buachaill*, a lad, or herdsman, is a likely source of that descriptive word for a wee roond Glaswegian, a bachle. The erosion of distinctively Scots vocabulary was also set in train, but the grammar and structure of the original dialect remained surprisingly intact. This was a double blow for the status of the city dialects; Victorian society dismissed Scots, but antiquarianism allowed that some of the words were expressive. However, the grammatical features of Scots which differed from English, eg we wes for we were, were condemned outright as slovenly English. Without the saving grace of the old words, but the so-called "slovenly English" intact, the town dialects were liked not a bit by the Establishment. As early as 1840 "a Babylonish dialect, both in idioms and in accent" has resulted in Lochwinnoch, Renfrewshire, and the blame, according to Andrew Crawfurd, lies with the influx of a "clanjamfray of Irish [and] Highlanders". Crawfurd stresses that " this corruption is alone in the village. . . The country part of the parish exhibits a pattern approaching to the Doric and chaste dialect". One of the shibboleths which most enraged the Establishment was the glottal stop, which seems to have originated in the Glasgow area and by association spread out over first the towns of the western Lowlands, and in our own century, to most of the towns of Scotland. Whether it came with the Irish immigrants, or was a result of the meeting of the immigrant's language and that of the native population, is difficult to ascertain. Whatever it was, pronounciations like wa'er, bu'er, Cel'ic still cause middle-class matrons to throw up their hands in horror. The reports of the school Inspectors are full of negative responses to the town dialects. Typical is this one from Lanarkshire in 1895 which pinpoints the abhorrant details:

> . . . the mutilation of final syllables, and especially the conversion of final d into t; the slurring over of intermediate consonants, and the omission of sibilants.

Safe in the knowledge that there was no fear of the traditional dialect coming back to the towns, the Inspectors and other members of the establishment begun contrasting the corruption of the city with the chasteness of the country dialects; they now felt they could attack from a purist English and Scots attitude. The falseness of their posture is revealed in the fact that in areas where the so-called corruption of the city had not penetrated, the local Inspectors were just as hostile to country dialects as their colleagues to the speech of the cities. An Inspector for the Northern district – about as far from the glottal stop as you could get – writing in 1895, regretted that teachers could not contribute more to the

> . . . scotching and eradicating of the horrible accent and vernacular in some parts of the North. . . a number of excrescent branches might usefully be lopped off. The tree would be none the worse for the operation.

The dialect which has long been regarded as the most unaffected, "chaste" and conservative Scots is that of Aberdeenshire. One of the North-East ministers who contributed to the Second

Statistical Account of 1845 had this to say about the rural dialect spoken there: "The most common dialect is a mixture of Scotch and English, the Scotch used being of the somewhat vicious kind, known, I believe, by the name of the Aberdeenshire". In other words, no matter what the local form of Scots is, you can be sure the local establishment will be hostile to it.

Yet, within that establishment itself there were undoubtedly many different styles of speech, especially in the first half of the century when many were still in a transition stage, trying to lose their Scots but not quite getting the hang of the English. Lord Braxfield, one of the Scots-speaking judges in Edinburgh, said of Francis Jeffrey of the *Edinburgh Review*, "The laddie has clean tint his Scotch, and found nae English." The anglified Scot obviously found little initial favour among his countrymen, as this snippet from the *Scots Magazine* of 1821 testifies; "The haill kintra gat begunkit wi an Yinglifiet jargon". Jeffrey's hybrid speech appears to hae gart baith friend an fae tak a grue at it. His foe, the Tory Lockhart, described his speech as: "A mixture of provincial English, with undignified Scotch, altogether snappish and offensive, and which would be quite sufficient to render the elocution of a more ordinary man utterly disgusting." Jeffrey may have spoken rather like what later became known as Morningsaide or Kelvinsaide, that peculiarly Scottish expression of over-refinement in speech. It is difficult to give an idea of this speech to non-Scots without using phonetic symbols: its most distinctive feature though is the attempt to "raise" broad Scottish vowels such as the a in back to something closer to e, giving the sound beck; this phenomenon gave rise to the old joke that sex are what Morningside ladies put their garbage in! Some linguists believe these accents to be throw-backs to the 18th-century period of Scots trying to learn London English; thus Kelvinside may preserve some fossilised aspects of London speech of the 1760s. Whatever it was, even Cockburn, Jeffrey's political ally and friend, lamented the strange affected hybrid that escaped his lips:

> It would have been better if he had merely got some of the grosser matter rubbed off his vernacular tongue, and left himself, unencumbered both by it and by unattainable English, to his own respectable Scotch, refined by literature and good society, and used plainly and naturally, without shame, and without affected exaggeration.

The feeling of revulsion this Anglo-Scottish hybrid produced among some sections of Scottish society – those who did not in fact speak it – was still strong in 1903. In his monumental work, *A Literary History of Scotland*, A.H. Millar followed the quote above by Cockburn with the words *dis aliter visum* (the Gods thought otherwise) and the regretful conclusion that

> Jeffrey has proved to be the ancestor of a numerous progeny, who, in the pulpit, in the law courts, or in private life, talk a mincing and quasi-genteel lingo of their own (the sort of English known in some quarters as "Princes Street" or "Kelvinside'), the subtly hideous *nuances* of which not the most elaborate system of phonetic spelling yet devised would suffice to reproduce.

Kelvinside eventually became the butt of so many jokes that it survives only in patches, and usually among the old. When Millar was writing, presumably something approaching the Scottish Standard English we recognise today had evolved and become established alongside Oxford English as an acceptable medium for "educated" Scots to communicate in. Even it would have its detractors, for it appears that every form of Scottish speech raises the hackles of one section of society or another, be it urban versus rural, Kelvinside versus Received Pronunciation, or glottal stop versus affectation; it is all part of a feeling of insecurity in the way we speak. If Lowland Scotland had once been a united linguistic commmunity, it was now one rent with prejudices based on class, locality and nationality; welcome to the modern world.

# Chapter 8

## Renaissance and Erosion

The status of Scots at the beginning of this century derived very much from trends established in the 18th century and hardened in the 19th century. The language came to be regarded as a working-class patois, despised by the increasingly anglicised upper and middle classes. To them, Scots was fine as a medium for couthy novels, newspaper cartoons, and music hall comedians. When radio, cinema newsreel, and television eventually came along the Scotch stereotypes established in the music halls by Harry Lauder and his like were adopted by media dominated by Englishmen who cared little about reflecting the real Scotland, and less about the cultural sensitivities of her people. Besides, the Scots swallowed the myths and stereotypes themselves.

The upper classes and sections of the upper middle class spoke now in a manner scarcely distinguishable from the English of the Home Counties. Scottish R.P. speakers may still pronounce the wh in whales to differentiate it from wales, and they may miss out the intrusive r in the Home Counties' 'Lawr and Order', but to the majority of Scots they are speaking with an English accent. Edinburgh, with certain of its fee-paying schools specialising in teaching R.P., produces more such speakers than any other town. In all the other towns and cities, Standard Scottish English rather than R.P. tends to be the medium favoured by the upper middle and middle class. Coming from the West of Scotland, where an English accent meant that the person was English, it came as a surprise to me at Edinburgh University that some Scots, and some patriotic Scots at that, could sound like Englishmen. The majority of Scots who are culturally anglicised, however, accept and rejoice in their anglicisation, for British society has conferred status on English culture, not Scottish. Those who speak Scots, and even many who speak Scottish English, resent the prestige of R.P.

and regard their countrymen who speak it, often erroneously, as cultural quislings. Strong feelings are raised on both sides of the linguistic divide in Scotland, and both the upper class and bourgeois contempt for Scots and the working class dislike of "posh English" are both reprehensible yet symptomatic of a country cut off from knowledge of its own cultural and linguistic history. Expressions of both sides' attitudes are easy to find, the former in official educations reports, the latter in literature. 19th century hostility to the vernacular on the part of the education authorities has continued, and in 1946 a Report on Primary Education described Scots in the following terms:

> the homely, natural and pithy everyday speech of country and small-town folk in Aberdeenshire and adjacent counties, and to a lesser extent in other parts outside the great industrial areas. But it is not the language of 'educated' people anywhere, and could not be described as a suitable medium of education or culture. Elsewhere because of extraneous influences it has sadly degenerated, and become a worthless jumble of slipshod ungrammatical and vulgar forms, still further debased by the intrusion of the less desirable Americanisms of Hollywood. . . Against such unlovely forms of speech masquerading as Scots we recommend that the schools should wage a planned and unrelenting campaign.

The result of this war of attrition, however, has not been an improvement in English, just a confusing resentment among those whose culture was the butt of this educational joke. Gordon Williams portrays well the linguistic confusion which the S.E.D. has wrought in this scene from his novel *From Scenes Like These*, where a young Ayrshire boy contemplates the speech of his environment.

> It was very strange how the old man changed accents. Sometimes he spoke to you in broad Scots, sometimes in what the school teachers called proper English. They were very hot on proper English at the school. Once he'd got a right showing up in the class for accidentally pronouncing butter 'bu'er'. Miss Fitzgerald had gone on (him having to stand in front of the class) about the glottal stop being dead common and very low-class, something that would damn you if you wanted a decent job. A decent job – like a bank! His mother spoke proper English, but then she was hellish keen on proving they were respectable. His father spoke common Kilcaddie, which he knew his mother didn't

like. When the Craigs spoke broad it wasn't quite the same as common Kilcaddie – some of their expressions sounded as though they came straight out of Rabbie Burns! Telfer had a Kilcaddie accent, but he pronounced all his words properly, no doubt from seeing too many pictures. McCann spoke very coarse and broad, but there was something false about him, as though he put it on deliberately.

He still spoke the school's idea of proper English, he knew that all right because every time he opened his mouth he could hear himself sounding like a real wee pan-loaf toff. (Maybe that was what annoyed McCann?) Why did auld Craig and Willie change about? Did it depend on what they thought about you? He remembered Nicol the English teacher saying that broad Scots was pronounced very much like Anglo-Saxon or middle English or some such expression. If that was so why did they try and belt you into speaking like some English nancy boy on the wireless? He'd asked Nicol that and Nicol said right or wrong didn't come into it, proper English was what the school had to teach you if you weren't going to be a guttersnipe all your life. Was it being a guttersnipe to talk your own country's language? It would be a lot healthier if folk spoke one way. Sometimes you hear them say "eight" and sometimes "eicht", sometimes "farm" and sometimes "ferm". Sometimes "ye" and sometimes "youse" and sometimes "yese" and sometimes "you". Sometimes "half" and sometimes "hauf". Was it your faither or your father? Your mither or your mother? He felt he was speaking to his audience again. You see, if school was any use it would teach you things like that, not jump on you for not talking like a Kelvinside nancy boy. Why teach kids that Burns was the great national poet and then tell you his old Scots words were dead common? What sounds better – "gie your face a dicht wi' a clootie" or "give your face a wipe with a cloth"? One was Scottish and natural and the other was a lot of toffee-nosed English shite.

If the conclusion is extreme, so are the circumstances which gave rise to the resentment. William McIlvanney explores the theme of identity conflict in his fine novel *Docherty*. In this extract, the boy Conn is brought before the Headmaster to be punished for fighting in the playground. The different linguistic identities of master and pupil are central to what ensues.

"...What's wrong with your face, Docherty?"
"Skint ma nose, sur."
"How?"
"Ah fell an' bumped ma heid in the sheuch, sur."
"I beg your pardon?"

"Ah fell an' bumped ma heid in the sheuch, sur."
"I beg your pardon?"
In the pause, Conn understands the nature of the choice tremblingly, compulsively, makes it.
"Ah fell an' bumped ma heid in the sheuch, sur."
The blow is instant. His ear seems to enlarge, is muffed in numbness. But it's only the dread of tears that hurts. Mr. Pirrie distends on a lozenge of light that mustn't be allowed to break. It doesn't. Conn hasn't cried.
"That, Docherty is impertinence. You will translate, please, into the mother-tongue."
The blow is a mistake, Conn knows. If he tells his father, he will come up to the school. "Ye'll take whit ye get wi' the strap an' like it. But if onybody takes their hauns tae ye, ye'll let me ken." He thinks about it. But the problem is his own. It frightens him more to imagine his father coming up.
"I'm waiting, Docherty. What happened?"
"I bumped my head, sir."
"Where? Where did you bump it, Docherty?"
"In the gutter, sir."
"Not an inappropriate setting for you, if I may say so."

Having received six strokes of the tawse, Conn goes back to his desk and works out what the incident means to him.

Relating to it, realignments were already taking place in him. . . He knew his father's contempt for the way they had to live and his reverence for education. But against that went Conn's sense of the irrelevance of school, its denial of the worth of his father and his family, the falsity of its judgements, the rarified atmosphere of its terminology.

By way of exorcising the pain, Conn compiles a list of words in the way he had seen in the dictionary.

| | |
|---|---|
| sheugh | gutter |
| speugh | sparrow |
| lum | chimney |
| brace | mantelpiece |
| bine | tub |
| coom | soot |
| coomie | foolish man (Mr. Pirrie) |
| gomeril | another foolish man |
| spicket | tap |
| glaur | muck what is in a puddle after the puddle goes away |

| wabbit | tired |
|---|---|
| whaup | curlew |
| tumshie | turnip |
| breeks | trousers |
| chanty | po |
| preuch | anything you can get |
| I was taigled longer | I was kept back for a longer |
| nor I ettled | time than I desired. |

One side of the paper was filled. He didn't start on the other because he now wanted to write things that he couldn't find any English for. When something sad had happened and his mother was meaning there wasn't anything you could do about it, she would say "ye maun dree yer wierd." When she was busy, she had said she was "saund-papered to a whippet." "Pit a raker oan the fire." "Hand-cuffed to Mackindoe's ghost." "A face to follow a flittin." If his father had to give him a row but wasn't really angry, he said "Ah'll skelp yer bum wi' a tea leaf tae your nose bluids."
Conn despaired of English. Suddenly with the desperation of a man trying to amputate his own infected arm, he savagely scored out all the English equivalents. On his way out of the school, he folded his grubby piece of paper very carefully and put it in his pocket, It was religiously preserved for weeks. By the time he lost it, he didn't need it.

McIlvanney is one of the most acute and articulate observers of Scottish society. The theme of working-class individuals and communities having to define their worth against hostile authorities and forces which have no regard for their culture is central to all his work. As a writer stemming from the people and expressing their culture, he is very much part of a Scottish tradition in literature which is quite different from that of England. There, literature has tended to be the preserve of an élite. The English Romantic poets were interested in the life of the common man, but they saw his culture as outsiders; Burns was from the people and wrote about them in their own tongue. In 'The Mother Tongue' McIlvanney summed up the difference in the two traditions, recalling his study of English Literature at Glasgow University:

when I went to the fabled fortress of learning, and realised, in my terms anyway, that what I was offered as literature excluded the majority of the people that I come from. . . it was like a body of evidence in which 98% of the witnesses are never called. And I don't think that's true of Scottish literature, there is a more radical demand throughout Scottish literature to allow the voice of those who may not write themselves to be validly heard.

Sir David Lyndsay in the 16th century, Robert Burns in the 18th century and numerous novelists, playwrights and poets of the 20th century testify to the radical tradition in Scottish, and specifically Scots literature which shows no sign of abating.

The man who created the climate for modern literature in Scots, was a radical Communist and Nationalist called Christopher Murray Grieve, alias Hugh MacDiarmid. Grieve was a native Scots speaker from Langholm near the English border; single-handedly he dragged Scots out of the couthy Kailyard to re-create it as a medium of poetry of international calibre. His method of doing this was novel; augmenting his native Scots with words from dictionaries, seeking words from different dialects and past ages of the language, and inventing words of his own where all else failed. What he did can be compared with Dante's achievement in creating a national tongue out of the welter of Italian dialects at the turn of the 14th century; MacDiarmid's achievement may be recognised in the same terms some day, but for the moment an anglicised Scotland is still getting over the shock of the despised patois being taken seriously internationally once again. While his long philosophical and political poems such as 'The Drunk Man Looks at the Thistle' and 'Second Hymn to Lenin' succeeded in raising and expanding the language's capabilities, and finally sweeping away the couthiness of the Kailyard, many feel his greatest poetic achievement lies in his early lyric poetry. 'The Watergaw' has the sensual feel and feyness of the great ballads.

> Ae weet forenicht i' the yow-trummle
> I saw yon antrin thing,
> A watergaw wi' its chitterin' licht
> Ayont the on-ding;
> An' I thocht o' the last wild look ye gied
> Afore ye deed
>
> There was nae reek i' the laverock's hoose
> That nicht – an' nane i' mine;
> But I hae thocht o' that foolish licht
> Ever sin' syne;

An' I think that mebbe at last I ken
What your look meant then.

(*watergaw* indistinct rainbow; *forenicht* early evening; *yow-trummle* cold weather after sheep-shearing (English- ewe tremble); *antrin* rare; *chitterin'* shivering; *on-ding* onset (of rain); *reek* smoke; *laverock* lark; *sin' syne* since then.

MacDiarmid's remarkable synthesis of Scots worked brilliantly, and he was followed by a strong group of poets including Douglas Young, Sidney Goodsir Smith, Robert Garioch, William Soutar, and Alexander Scott, all part of a Renaissance which is still influencing writers today. The synthesis called variously Lallans (an alternative name for Scots used by Burns), Plastic Scots and Synthetic Scots provoked tremendous debate, and twenty one years after the publication of MacDiarmid's first collection 'Sangschaw', the *Glasgow Herald's* letter pages were still thrang with arguments for and against the Scots of the new makars. The *Herald* tended to patronise or ridicule the movement, and fuel the controversy with comments in its editorial diary such as this one for November 9, 1946.

It is, of course, much easier to write plastic Scots than to read it, and the art can easily be mastered with the help of a few simple rules. . . Manner is your concern rather than matter. Your subjects need be few – Hugh MacDiarmid, Glasgow, the Highlands, the English, love, drink, and Hugh MacDiarmid. You should write at least one ode to Hugh MacDiarmid: this is *de rigueur*. After all, he invented synthetic Scots, from which the plastic form is derived. It is not necessary for what you write to have no meaning, but it is vital to conceal your meaning, if any, as much as possible

The main objection to Lallans was the fact that it used words which were not in current usage, and therefore the literature produced in it was artificial. The fact that every writer in the history of literature in any language has used words not in current usage never entered the heads of the detractors – bourgeois Scots in the main, who knew as much about current usage in Scots as in Japanese. Sidney Goodsir Smith gave an apt reply to this criticism in his 'Epistle to John Guthrie' (who had blamed the poet for writing in Scots 'which no one speaks').

We've come intil a gey queer time

Whan scrievin Scots is near a crime,
'There's no one speaks like that', they fleer,
– But wha the deil spoke like King Lear?

(*scrievin* writing; *fleer* sneer).

One or two people did write in Scots because it was fashionable for a while to do so, and not being native speakers, there is a certain stilted labouring in their attempts to convince in Scots. For the majority of the poets and playwrights however, they were extending a language intimately familiar to them. In a letter to the *Glasgow Herald* dated November 13, 1946, MacDiarmid stresses this very point. Having dismissed the quality of Scottish poetry in English, he goes on:

> What, then, is the Scottish poet to do but try to extend and strengthen his own native language in precisely the way that all languages, including English, have extended and strengthened themselves – and that is all synthetic Scots has attempted! It is not the case that modern Scots poets have invented new words to eke out their vocabulary. Nor is it the case that they have had undue recourse to Jamieson's Dictionary. Most of them write on the solid basis of the speech they first spoke as children and were familiar with in their homes – the speech, incidentally, of the vast majority of the Scottish working class, still, and, judging by the scant headway made against it by English during the past two centuries, likely to remain so!

The prejudice against non-current Scots is, I believe, part of the Establishment's death wish, and it arises in the spoken as well as the written tongue. No one blinks an eye if you use English, French or German words you learn from books or dictionaries, yet come out with a Scots word ye didnae learn at yer mither's knee and you are accused of using language 'artificially.' Literature has always gone beyond the everyday language, the nature of poetry especially being to extend our linguistic experience. Nevertheless, I have often been surprised to hear words being used naturally by Scots speakers in different parts of the country, which I presumed MacDiarmid had got out of the dictionary. This supports his contention that most of the vocabulary he uses was actually current in the time he wrote. Coming from a fairly strong Scots-speaking area, I presumed that if a word was not used in my own dialect, it would also have become obsolete elsewhere. In 'The Watergaw' for example forenicht, chitterin, reek and laverock were all familiar to me, but yow-trummle, antrin, and watergaw were not. Since I first read the poem though, I have discovered that antrin is an everyday word in the North-East, yow trummle is known in the Borders, and when making 'The Mother Tongue', a girl from my own Irvine Valley related that watergaw was a word her grandmother used. Being brought up in the early part of the century before the erosion of Scots vocabulary initiated by radio and television set in, MacDiarmid must have heard many of these words which appear as exotic to us, every day in life.

Scots has been fragmented as a language, and with the dearth of broadcasting in the remaining dialects, very few people have first-hand experience of the spectrum of Scots which is spoken across the country. Many subscribe to the Establishment's desire to destroy the language, unaware that a few miles down the road it is being spoken in all its vigour and power. For despite the erosion, a remarkable amount of Scots survives, and in the unlikeliest places.

Once, talking about Scots to a class of teenagers in Pilton, a big housing scheme in Edinburgh, I was astonished that a number of the kids knew and used the word partan for a crab. It had long disappeared from my own dialect. The reason for its survival in Pilton was the fact that the kids frequent Cramond shore, which is within walking distance, and they heard the word used by fishermen there. The word wapinschaw, a muster of arms, is another word from Medieval Scots, mentioned by Scott in *Old Mortality*, which one presumes died long ago. Yet it is a word in common use among the bowling fraternity in the West of Scotland, describing a competition day when one club plays against another.

Having had the good fortune to travel around Scotland for 'The Mother Tongue', 'The Scots Tongue' and 'Odyssey', I can testify to the smeddum that's still in the auld leid. I recall Evelyn Crockett of Lossiemouth coming out with classical Scots sentences such as the following in her description of life at the herring gutting: "We uised tae hain a puckle stanes tae fleg awa the gows" – we used to keep a few stones to frighten away the seagulls. And it isn't just old folk who have command of

Scots; this was how a sixteen-year-old from Ayrshire described the domestic chores her mother asked her to do following the family's tea: "Well she'd tell ye tae gae ben the kitchen, an it wad be in a mogre wi aw the creishie cups an dishes. An she'd say 'turn on the spicket an synd oot thae dishes, then dicht roon the sink.' I wad breenge aboot tryin tae pit everythin bye..an the dog wad be cooerin in the corner, feart in case I skelpit it for gettin in the wye!" Yet so conditioned are we to thinking of Scots as a dying language, that even after hearing concentrated articulate Scots like these examples above, many would still say, "Oh that's guid Scots, but ye ken, it's deein oot!" The overriding propaganda against Scots has resulted even in Scots speakers believing and taking part in the destruction the authorities have wished on the language for over two hundred years. The working class continue speaking Scots, and if there is a slow erosion of the distinctive Scots vocabulary with every generation, it still remains very much the spoken language of the people. Because of that fact, the other social classes are intimately familiar with it. How else could this 'dead or dying' language be such a successful medium for the theatre? In the past year I have seen *The Wallace* by Sidney Goodsir Smith, *Ane Satyre of the Thrie Estaitis* by Sir David Lyndsay, *The Flouers o' Edinburgh* by Robert McLellan, Moliere's *Tartuffe* rendered brilliantly into Scots by Liz Lochhead and my own play *They Fairly Mak Ye Work* at Dundee Rep: all of these plays were in Scots and every one of them played to packed appreciative audiences whose response spoke volumes on the myth of incomprehensibility and the myth of the language being obsolete and dying. The people speak it, and sing it – for folk-song is another area where Scots has remained strong and popular – the writers write it, the audience understands it. It's no deid yet! It's time the claith wes pit ower that particular claikin parrot!

Liz Lochhead's *Tartuffe* is particularly exciting because it succeeds in fusing the contemporary urban idiom with the more classical Scots established by Robert Kemp and Robert McLellan earlier this century. It is a fusion that works, proving that modern Glaswegian for example can blend with more traditional Scots. It is a pointer to what could and should happen in the future. For Scots literature must retain its raw, radical political edge if it is to be relevant to future generations. That edge is to be found in the work of certain Glasgow writers such as James Kelman and Tom Leonard. Influenced by the American poet William Carlos Williams who sought to write in American speech rhythms, Leonard's poetry seeks to express a variety of Glasgow voices. It registers more when heard than read. In 'Unrelated Incidents – 3' the satire on language and power is direct and very much to the point.

> this is thi
> six a clock
> news thi
> man said n
> thi reason
> a talk wia
> BBC accent
> iz coz yi
> widny wahnt
> mi ti talk
> aboot thi
> trooth wia
> voice lik
> wanna yoo
> scruff. if
> a toktaboot
> thi trooth
> lik wanna yoo
> scruff yi
> widny thingk
> it waz troo.
> jist wanna yoo
> scruff tokn.
> thirza right
> way ti spell
> ana right way
> ti tokit. this
> is me tokn yir
> right way a
> spellin. this
> is ma trooth.
> yooz doant no
> thi trooth
> yirsellz cawz
> yi canny talk
> right. this is
> the six a clock
> nyooz. belt up.

Purists of both the Scots and English language have criticised the Glasgow dialect, and Leonard's reproduction of it – suggesting he should join one side or the other. With his stress on the voice – the actuality of what people say – language prescription of any kind is anathema to him and is given short shrift. In one poem a man who accepts that 'thi langwij a thi guhtr' is o.k. for comic poetry, but is useless for expressing serious concerns, symbolically falls down a lift shaft.

Very different in style from the city poets but retaining their social commitment, Scots has also been the medium of the great folksong revival which took place in the 1950s and still affects popular culture in the 1980s. Hamish Henderson is one of the major figures of the revival, both for his discovery and recording of great tradition-bearers such as Jeannie Robertson and for the tremendous emotive impact of his Scots lyrics in political songs such as 'The Freedom Come All Ye':

> O come all ye at hame wi' freedom,
> Never heed whit the hoodies croak for doom;
> In your hoose a' the bairns o' Adam
> Can find breid, barley bree an painted room.
> When Maclean meets wi's freens in Springburn
> A' the roses an' geans will turn tae bloom,
> And a black boy frae yont Nyanga
> Dings the fell gallows o' the burghers doon.

> (*hoodies* crows; *barley bree* whisky; *geans* wild cherries.)

While poetry, drama and song in a range of different styles of Scots thrives in the 20th century, the same cannot be said of literature in prose. With no tradition since the 17th century to act as models, writers have until very recently been wary of attempting prose in Scots of any length. Spurred by the Scots Language Society and its quarterly magazine *Lallans*, however, the last decade has seen an expansion of prose writing in Scots. Short stories where the narrator is a Scots speaker are certainly the most successful attempts – Robert McLellan's 'Linmill' stories are excellent by any standard. Expository prose is altogether more difficult – with no precedent to prepare one for it, even the Scots speaker finds lines such as the following strange to the eye; "Lallans is publisht bi the Scots Language Society, wi the help o siller frae The Scottish Arts Council".

Once you are used to the conventions, however, the Scots prose of *Lallans* can appear quite natural and fluent. Writers such as Alexander Scott, J.K. Annand, Donald Campbell and William Neill have all contributed tremendous energy to the advancement of the Scots language cause, and are to be applauded for their efforts in re-establishing models for prose in the language. J.K. Annand's bairn-rhymes are weel kent, but here is an example of his prose in Scots, the opening paragraph of an obituary he wrote on a fellow makar in *Lallans*, Mairtinmas, 1985.

> Robert McLellan was a Lanarkshire callant. His faither was John McLellan, brocht up in Lanark, a prenter to tred, that was merrit on Elizabeth Hannah, dochter of a fritt fermer frae nearby Kirkfieldbank. Whan they set up hous they baid at 14 Ferguson Avenue, Milngavie. Whan her time cam, his mither, as was the wey o't in thae days afore the National Health, gaed hame til her mither for the lyin-in. And sae it cam aboot that Robert McLellan was born at Linmill on the twinty-eicht o Janwar 1907. (The place is spelt Linnmill nouadays, but Robert aye threipit that Linmill was the richt spellin, eftir the lint or flax that was aince wrocht there, and had nocht to dae wi the nearby linns o Clyde.) In his bairnheid he spent a lot o time at Linmill wi his grannie and grandfaither, and the ongauns there were aa grist til his mill whan he cam in later days to scrieve his Linmill stories.

No matter what you feel about Scots prose, the fact is that the on-going Renaissance in literature in Scots has undoubtedly helped towards raising the status and prestige of the language, written and spoken. The success of 20th-century literature in Scots has forced the schools and universities to take Scots seriously once again. This still falls far short of the status an integral part of a national culture should have within education in its native land; but with courses on Scots taught at Aberdeen, Edinburgh and Glasgow Universities and the literature expanding throughout Scottish education, the language and culture undoubtedly enjoy more prestige today than for many a long year. The Association for Scottish Literary Studies publishes much of the good work going on in the universities in its journals and actively promotes Scottish studies within Scottish society. The Linguistic Survey of Scotland, the Scottish National Dictionary Association, the Dictionary of the Older

Scottish Tongue, the School of Scottish Studies, the Country Life Archive of the National Museum, the Saltire Society all contribute their bit towards creating a climate whereby Scottish culture is slowly gaining the recognition it merits at home and abroad.

Will Scots expand, or will it move closer and closer to English? Either option is possible. There is certainly enough Scots remaining familiar to most of us, that with language planning and the backing of a sympathetic education authority, there is no philological reason why Scots should not rise like Icelandic or Norwegian from being regarded as provincial dialects, to becoming full-blown national languages, regarded as such the world over. The language planning for a Standard Scots is already in motion with linguists such as J Derrick McClure, David Purves and A J Aitken having committed their ideas in print. If the very idea seems far-fetched, it seemed just that way to millions in countries where languages have been revived. All that is lacking here is the will. For the moment though, Standard Scots as an official language of Scotland is a million miles away – most of us would settle in the short term for our children being taught Scottish culture one period a week in the schools.

## Chapter 9

## *Wha's Like Us?*

"Here's tae us, wha's like us? – damned few an they're a' deid" runs the Scot's favourite toast to his own folk. The swagger implicit in the rhetorical question brooks no reply – we are the people and there is nothing and no one remotely like us in all the world! As far as language is concerned, however, there are millions of people like us in that they too live in states which give only grudging status, if any at all, to the language of so-called minorities within their borders. If we could break out of our landlocked British insular mentality and look as we did in the past to mainland Europe, we would find parallels to the Scots/English duality in almost every European country. We would also be astonished to discover that in certain geo-political circumstances, the disadvantaged status of Scots is paralleled by languages such as German and French, which appear to us as pillars of the European linguistic establishment. As I have shown already, one nation's language is another's corrupt dialect if a political border happens to be drawn in the wrong place. Europe, past and present, offers many varying parallels to the situation of Scots in Scotland – some pessimistic and others extremely optimistic. Ignorance about how language evolves is at the heart of much of the prejudice against languages which differ from the principal standard variety in e.g. Britain, France and Spain. Many speakers of Standard English, French and Castilian Spanish actually believe that their language has existed unchanged as a pillar of perfection for centuries, and that e.g. Scots, Occitan, and Catalan are aberrant corruptions of this perfection, perpetrated by the irrational thrawnness and innate barbarity of the peoples in question. I have heard people in France and Iberia come away with the same hoary old chestnuts that you hear in Scotland: "the people of Catalonia/ Occitania do not speak a language but a ragbag of a dialect that takes the worst from French and Spanish and mixes them together in an uncouth manner to create an unintelligible patois which should be consigned to the trash can". That the *langue d'oc* and Catalan, like Scots, have brilliant literary traditions and have been spoken in their homelands for centuries, these people know not and care not a jot. They have a world picture and they are sticking to it, even if it is wrong-headed.

France of course has been the most centralised of European states for a long time. Historically there were two major language groups within French, the *langue d'oil* of the north, and the *langue d'oc* of the south. When political control of a unified French state became centred in Paris, the southern language, like that of the Breton, Basque and Catalan people, was regarded as inimical to the unity of the country and so the state sought to impose Northern French on all of these areas. As early as 1539 an ordinance of King Francis I declared this French as the only official language of the realm. The erosion of the *langue d'oc*, also known as Occitan or Provençal, proceeded apace, much like the erosion of Scots following the Union of the Crowns. Napoleon's concept of *liberté égalité and fraternité* also had dire consequences for the other native languages of France. To be truly *égale* or equal, the Revolution decided, everyone had to share the same cultural identity and speak the same language. The languages of the so-called minorities were to be rooted out, and in tones reminiscent of the Scottish Augustans, denounced as 'un reste de barbarie des siècles passés' The people themselves who speak dialects descended from the Provençal of the Troubadours, have been indoctrinated by the state to regard their speech as a corruption of French. In the south of France, as with Scotland, however, an intermittently brilliant literature in the Occitan language has continued and the Provençal equivalent of Hugh MacDiarmid was the poet Frédéric Mistral (1830-1914). He recreated the dialects into a vibrant literary language and initiated a Renaissance in the culture of the south of France. There also arose a parallel autonomist political movement, as was the case with most of the deposed linguistic and national groups in Europe. Today, in the area of the *langue d'oc* there is a population of 15 million, of whom roughly ten million have some knowledge of Occitan and two million, mainly in the rural areas, use it as their everyday language of communication. Like those who speak a full canon of Scots, all Occitan-speakers also are able to switch to their language of education, the *langue d'oil* or Standard French, with comparative ease.

Catalonia is a nation in the North-East corner of Iberia. Her language, Catalan spills over into the French province of Roussillon, and is spoken in the Balearic Islands, with enclaves in far-flung places such as Sardinia in Italy. Despite suppression and banning by the Spanish authorities at various times in its history, especially during the Franco years, Catalan is still the language of over five million people of all social classes in both town and country. The term "minority language" is one invented by the nation state which wants to diminish the status of a language. In the public mind it conjures up images of peasants talking to their stirks in a quaint patois up some sleepy hollow where time stands still. Nothing could be further from the truth as far as Catalan is concerned; it is spoken by intellectuals, industrialists, artists and artisans in one of the most sophisticated and cultured cities of Europe, Barcelona. Catalan gives living testimony to the importance of the survival of language among the people whose culture it expresses. The higher echelons of Catalan society had turned to Castilian as the language of court as early as the 15th century, and much of the best writing was in Castilian – a parallel to the Scots situation following the Union of the Crowns. The fortunes of the language waxed and waned, with literary and cultural revivals followed by periods when the language appeared to be moribund and the country succumbing more and more to Spanish influence. It may have been the suppression of the culture itself which made the language a symbol of resistance and gave the people a focus for retaining it. Franco's victory in 1936 lead to the banning of it in public, and until recently it was not even taught in Barcelona University. But the popular resistance was such that today, with a degree of political autonomy, the Catalans have their own Catalan television service and the language is represented at every phase of the area's life. According to the Spanish government of a decade ago, Catalan did not exist.

European linguistic boundaries predate political borders. Political borders are extremely changeable and even our present century has witnessed several radical changes in the map of Europe as a result of two world wars. Linguistic communities tend to have roots in their native regions which go back hundreds of years, and although political change can suddenly affect the fortunes of a language, the change in the native spoken vernacular tends to be slow. In the case of long-established political borders which run through a distinctive linguistic community, the effect is rather on the status of the language spoken on either side of the national frontier. The northern border of Portugal with Spain provides graphic illustration of the effect of politics on the status and prestige of language. The people to the south and north of the River Minho speak the same language. In the south it is called Portuguese and has the prestige and kudos of a national and international language spoken from Lisbon to Luanda in Angola, from Rio de Janeiro in Brazil to Timor in the East Indies. To the north it is called Galician and is regarded as a provincial dialect or "bad Spanish" by the Spanish state, who have imposed their own standard dialect as the medium of education and the media, rather like English in Scotland. Because of the erosion that inevitably follows from such policies, Galician did not evolve to cope with the demands of modern society like her sister language Portuguese. Because of that, however, it retains many older features which have died out in Portuguese, again like Scots in relation to Old English. For the Galician people, though, it is still a powerful focus for their strong Celtic identity and a vehicle for their best poetry and song. Galician today is in the same kind of condition as Scots, but politics could easily have placed Portuguese in the same precarious position. For at the time Scots came under threat towards the end of the 16th century, Portuguese came under political threat as the Spanish occupied the country for sixty years and began to impose their culture on the country. If the Portuguese had not succeded in kicking out the occupying power, Portugal would have been like Catalonia or Galicia today, its language regarded by the world as corrupt Spanish.

The indivisible link that European states have established between themselves and their principal languages is one that belies the complexity of the continent's linguistic heritage. Rather than accepting cultural diversity as a source of vitality and strength, the nation states have continuously attempted to deny the existence of the multiplicity of ethnic languages and dialects within their territories. Their thinking has conditioned us all: the word language is frequently associated with the speech of a sovereign national state, while the word dialect is associated with a regional variation of the national language. Yet all languages are dialects, all dialects language. All speech is part of a continuum determined often by the settlement of linguistic groups in a defined area many hundreds of years ago. Some of these dialects, that of the Paris basin or the East Midlands in England, for example, evolved into their national standard, but not because they were in any way superior to the other dialects surrounding them. The prestige of dialects has always been determined by political status – and historical accident.

The connection between language survival and political power is seen clearly when you examine the fate of the languages of the great nation states, when they happen to find themselves separated from the fatherland which nurtures them. Suddenly the giants of Europe's linguistic map come under threat, classified as remote provincial patois which run counter to the drive for national unity. This has been the case in this present century with the French and German languages within the Italian state. The French-speaking Val d'Aosta and German-speaking South Tyrol are historically part of the Alpine provinces of French *Savoie* and Austrian *Tyrol* respectively. The Aosta Valley was joined to Italy in 1860. The new Italian Republic was to be *una ed indivisible* and set about banning the native French, first from the schools in 1879 and then from the law courts in 1880. Mussolini's fascists prohibited the use of French in any sector of public life, including newspapers, speeches, place names and even personal names. With the advent of industry and tourism, Italians flooded into the area as permanent settlers. Rather like "white settlers" in the Scottish Gaidhealtachd, the incomers exercise tremendous influence on the communities they "invade" and with the backing of the state's propaganda, help erode the linguistic confidence of the native population. Since regional differences were recognised, on paper at least, by the Italian authorities in 1948 there has been a softening of attitude, and the schools teach French. But the process of italianisation proceeds unchecked. In 1901 in a population of 83,500, only 6,700 were Italian-speakers. Today half of the population speaks only Italian. The story is similar in South Tyrol, which was part of the German-speaking world for 14 centuries until its annexation by Italy following the Treaty of St Germain in 1919. Previously the province had approximately 233,000 German-speakers and 7,000 Italian-speakers. Today the balance is rather different with native German-speakers numbering 26,000 among a total population of 433,215. Since the Autonomy Statute of 1972, however, the native population have finally gained some degree of control over their destiny and for the first time there appears to be creative co-operation between province and state. If genuine bilingualism is established, South Tyrol may yet show Europe the strengths of a multicultural approach to the needs of her minorities. As European nation states bind themselves closer politically, the resistance to other cultures within the states should soften and *l'Europe des cent drapeaux* become a reality. Then perhaps all of Europe's deposed nations can enjoy the status of equality with the language and culture of the dominant group within the nation states.

All languages, from deposed national tongues like Catalan and Scots, to politically 'misplaced' languages like French and German, can come under threat if the government decides that their continuation is inimical to the cultural solidarity of the state. It would however be naive to think that national autonomy for the deposed language groups would automatically lead to the full restoration of the tongue to its original glory. Few nationalist movements bound themselves so closely to the restoration of their native language as did the Irish earlier this century. Since 1919 and the creation of the Free State in 1922, Irish Gaelic has been granted the status of "the first official language" and the compulsory teaching of Gaelic in school has resulted in the expansion of the numbers who have some command of the language, with over 25% of the population declaring knowledge of Irish in the census of 1971 – close on 800,000 people. For the vast majority of these people, however the knowledge of Irish is similar to the average Scot's knowledge of the French he was taught at school – no very guid. The actual number of people who use Irish as their everyday medium of communication is probably no more than 30,000, concentrated in the far west of the country in the government-funded official *Gaeltacht*. There, despite financial support, subsidised industry and successful local radio stations broadcasting in the language, the actual numbers of Irish-speakers is rapidly declining. For the linguistic anglicisation of Ireland has had its own in-built momentum for four centuries, and the people's association of the language with poverty and backwardness has not been eradicated with the alternative world picture on offer from Dublin. Irish Gaelic is probably in as perilous a position as Scottish Gaelic today, despite their very different status within their respective countries.

If the failure to re-establish Irish on the same level as English offers a salutary lesson to the wishful-thinking nationalist, there exist nevertheless spectacular examples of language revival against all the odds. At the end of the 19th century, when the first wave of Zionist immigrants were arriving in Palestine to put down the roots which developed into the State of Israel, Hebrew was all but a dead language. It's use, like Latin in the Catholic Church, was confined to religious worship, while the Jewish people spoke mainly Yiddish or the vernacular of the various European countries which had been their homelands for centuries. One of the first Jewish settlers in Palestine was a Lithuanian philologist born Eliezer Perlmann. On his arrival in the promised land in 1882, Perlmann changed his name to Ben Yehuda, and probably to the consternation of his wife and family, refused to speak anything but Hebrew. He helped re-invent the language, coining new words and preparing a moribund tongue for the modern world. By the 1890s this "new" Hebrew was being taught in the Jewish schools. Today it is the language of all Israelis. Now admittedly, few ethnic groups have been galvanised by terrible adversity like the Jews, and there is nothing typical about their experience. What the story does demonstrate is that if the will is there, even dead languages will revive and thrive. Scots is far from being a dead language. The parallels between Scots, Hebrew and Irish, however, are not as relevant as those between, for example, Scots and Catalan, or Occitan. The closeness and similarity of Scots to English, Catalan to Castilian Spanish and Occitan to French, has been a source of weakness and a potential source of strength. The erosion of Scots is more subtle and gradual because, so much being already shared with English, many are unaware where Scots stops and English starts. The style-switching and -drifting that most Scots engage in show just how easy it is to adapt from one language to the other. If the will existed to expand

and extend Scots, in other words, this would not present any great difficulty to the majority of the population. All they would have to overcome would be their social prejudices. On the other hand, the decline of completely different languages, e.g. Breton in France, Gaelic in Britain, Basque in Spain and Irish in Ireland, has a final and possibly irrevocable nature. These languages die out where they come into contact with the major language, then gradually the erosion eats into the heartland – the situation in the *Gaeltacht* of Ireland today. Catalan, and Occitan have not died. As J Derrick McClure put it, like Scots, they have "merely been pushed into a limbo of confusion and prejudice" at various points in their history.

The same could be said of Low German, today regarded as a provincial dialect of Northern Germany, but once the distinctive international lingua franca of the Hanseatic League. High German replaced it as the formal language of the area in a manner not unlike the advance of English against Scots. In some aspects Scots has fared better than Low German, with its more vibrant literature and with writers such as Burns and Scott who have made the language known in the rest of Britain, and the world. Low German literature has never travelled beyond its linguistic province, and has generally been ignored in the rest of Germany. But the German-speaking world is not as centralised linguistically and speakers of Low German are a lot less self-conscious about using their tongue in public; it is in common use in the church for example. The Germans have never regarded a strong dialect as standing in opposition to a strong national standard. This is borne out even more strongly in the case of Swiss German. To the ears of those raised on High German, Swiss German sounds rather like Buchan Doric to a lady from the Home Counties. Backed by their government, media, and strong sense of national identity, however, the Swiss are completely at home with their national form of German. They are taught to read and write in High German, and can speak it to communicate with foreigners, but they see no earthly reason to abandon their native tongue for the "foreign" standard one. Scots English too is a national form of a world language, but when you include the historical Scots elements in any comparison with other European linguistic dualities, more valid comparisons present themselves. The German philologist Manfred Görlach in a

paper comparing the fates of Scots and Low German, states:
". . . Scots was and is more removed from English than is the
case with modern pairs such as Czech and Slovak, Serbian and
Croatian, Bulgarian and Macedonian, or Swedish, Danish and
Norwegian – all of which are considered independent languages
by their speakers and in consequence, by linguists."

Scandinavia has long been held up by Scottish Nationalists
as a model for what the British Isles could be; a confederation
of sovereign nations mutually bound together through
common historical and cultural ties. The linguistic situation
in Scandinavia too provides stimulating parallels to the
Scots/English situation in Scotland. Danish, Norwegian,
Swedish, Icelandic and Faroese form a language continuum,
and with a modicum of good will, each can understand
the other's language. At one time Norwegian, Icelandic and
Faroese were regarded as dialects of Danish in the same way
as Scots is mistakenly regarded as a dialect of English today.
From the middle of the 15th century onwards, Danish came
to dominate Norwegian society. No Bible was produced
in Norwegian, and as in Scotland, this led to the decline of
the native vernacular as a written and eventually a spoken
medium among the upper classes. Even after Norway gained
independence from Denmark in 1814, Danish continued
unquestioned as the written and spoken language of power
and authority. During its long history in Norway, however,
the language adapted somewhat to local circumstances, and
*bokmål*, the name the Norwegians give this Dano-Norwegian
language is in a similar position to Scottish Standard English
today. However, while *bokmål* became the language of the
élite and eventually of the cities, the country districts held on
to their traditional Norwegian dialects. These dialects were
the basis of Ivar Aasen's remarkable attempt to intervene in
the erosion of the native vernacular, and through language-
planning and concern for the native culture, he succeeded in
creating *landsmål*, an alternative national language. The same
phenomenon occurred at different times in Iceland and the
Faroes, where philologists rebuilt a standard language for the
country out of the historical native vernacular. In Iceland,
and the Faroes the attempt was entirely successful and both
countries have vibrant thriving cultures in languages that at
one time were under the same threat that English poses for

Scots. In Norway the establishment of *landsmål*, also known as *nynorsk*, as an alternative national standard has only been partly successful. It has had a set grammar from 1864 and has enjoyed official status in the country since 1885. Communities can choose which of the national standards they prefer. In the populous east of the country and in the cities, the prestige of *bokmål* has remained unchanged. In the west and midlands of the country where the traditional dialects had been strongest, *landsmål* is the preferred standard for all aspects of life. About a sixth of Norwegian schoolchildren are taught in the language today. Although a minority tongue, it has a thriving literature and is understood perfectly and comprehensively by those who use *bokmål*. There is however an element of snobbism attached to the 'higher, foreign' register, and Magde Oftedal's remarks are also relevant to some English speakers' attitude to Scots in Scotland: "If some *bokmål* people claim not to understand Nynorsk, it is only pretence. It is the usual expedient of making a virtue out of ignorance, with the added ingredient that in this case the ignorance is not even genuine." *Landsmål*, because of the status it has enjoyed, has also influenced *bokmål* irrevocably, revitalising it with the vigour of the native speech.

Scots could be revived on a similar basis to *landsmål*, if the will existed. As we have seen with *landsmål* the extension of the native dialects into a codified standard was good not only for the native language but for the dominant language itself. I feel you could have the same kind of fertile fusion between Scots and English. But another important effect of all this language activity in countries like Norway is to heighten awareness of language itself. The Scandinavians are among the best and most natural linguists in the world. Belonging to small nations, they understand the necessity of communicating in other languages and with other cultures. They have long known that there is no tension between being local, national and international. That is another lesson we Scots could learn to our advantage.

# Chapter 10

## The Dialects of Scots

Because Scots does not have a recognised standard spoken form today, many believe that the various dialects spoken in Scotland are dialects of English. They are in fact dialects of Scots and form an unbroken continuum with the language which was the national tongue of the Middle Ages. The speech of someone from a conservative Scots-speaking area such as west Angus for example, has not changed a great deal in the intervening centuries; if time travel were feasible, a courtier speaking the Standard Lothian Scots of the 15th century would have little difficulty communicating with a contemporary Angus chield. The major dialect divisions of Scots have existed since the days when it was the national tongue, but these divisions were rarely reflected in the writing of the period. Writers wrote in a standard literary Scots, even if this did not reflect exactly the way they spoke. For example by the 16th century, people in the North-East already pronounced the sound wh as in 'what' with an f, giving the modern dialect spelling fat or fit in the area; but at that time writers in the region used the Standard Scots spelling quh or wh, giving quhat, or quhair. The reason we know that the f was already in the spoken tongue of the North East lies in the fact that in a few rare instances in the records, the scribe "slips up" and represents the sound in his writing – the exception proving the rule. In Walter Cullen's *Chronicle of Aberdeen*, he describes seeing James VI in 1580: ". . . I paist to Dunnottar, fair I beheld his graice". Normally the different spoken dialects were not reflected in the writing, and the literary standard was in use all over Scotland – a standard written language which everyone could understand.

Nowadays, of course, things are very different. With the decline of Scots as the national language, a sign of its fragmentation is the fact that for many Scots speakers and writers the local dialect is more important, and more clearly defined as an entity than something called Scots. This has had the beneficial effect of giving people pride in local culture and history, and encouraging writers to compose in a local form of Scots. But it has also produced the erroneous idea that the vernaculars of Buchan, Shetland or Dundee for example are unrelated, isolated in their own locality and different from all others when in fact they are all regional dialects of the same Scots tongue. This phenomenon is illustrated by the plethora of articles and books that have been published to satisfy local interest in the dialects, but which obscure the national dimension of the language. In the *Aberdeen Press and Journal* on March 27, 1986, for example, an article on North-East speech had the following under the title 'North-east Sayings':"aul' farrant, fair fleggit, fair forfochen, sleekit, scunnert, trauchelt". Now every one of these is common Scots, and would be known by most Scots-speakers. I have seen the same thing in lists of Dundonese vocabulary which include words like hirple, humff, halikit, and hurdies; in the *Shetland Dictionary* with words such as bide, birl, and ben; in Glasgow glossaries with Glaswegian words such as neb, neeps and noak. In almost every one of these, the fact that 90% of the words are common Scots is played down, and the uniqueness of the local dialect played up. That is not to say that every dialect does not have its unique vocabulary, as we shall see, but genuinely local words are the exception rather than the rule. Even in Shetland and Orkney, where Scots replaced the Scandinavian tongue Norn, the core vocabulary of the dialect is still general Scots with an admixture of Scandinavian words which are unique to the dialects of the Northern Isles.

The local focus and loyalty to the dialect is also determined by social factors. People are conditioned to switch to English in formal situations, so that Scots-speaking strangers will naturally communicate, at least initially, in English. The isolation of the dialects is also heightened by lack of exposure in the media – if people became accustomed to hearing the different dialects, they would quickly realise the similarities rather than fear the differences. The myth that Scots is only intelligible within a short radius and that one dialect speaker cannot communicate with another one from a different area has also resulted in a reduction in the use of Scots and a reinforcing of the local rather than the national identity with the tongue. I have heard many Scots-speakers say that they are only comfortable talking Scots to someone from the same locality. With everyone conditioned to some extent by official disdain for the tongue, it takes a strong person to speak Scots in a formal situation where people may classify them according to one or other stereotype as coarse or uneducated; it is so much simpler to speak English and save yourself the hassle.

Today, with mass communication influencing speech in every part of the country, the dialect differences are not nearly as great as they were even fifty years ago. Then towns a few miles apart, such as Galston and Darvel in my own area, spoke with recognisably different twangs. Nowadays, you can have accents that are frequently broadcast such as Glaswegian, influencing children's speech in Lerwick and Fort William, not to mention places nearer by. The distinction are slowly becoming blurred, but the major dialect divisions still prevail and can be detected immediately when you move from one area to another; the alert football fan, for example will notice a result of 2-1 given as twaw-wan in Glasgow, twa-ane in Dundee, and twae-yin in Lothian. According to the *Scottish National Dictionary*, the main dialect divisions are Insular Scots (Orkney and Shetland), Northern Scots, Mid or Central Scots and Southern Scots. Within these major divisions, there are many regional variations and dialect subdivisions as we shall see when we outline the features of the individual dialects more closely. For the sake of geographic precision, I have used the county references in the *Scottish National Dictionary* to pinpoint the dialect boundaries, rather than relate the dialects to the Regions and Districts which came into being in 1975. With over two-thirds of the population of Scotland, and the dialect from which the standard literary language derives, Central Scots deserves first place in any discussion on the dialects of Scots.

## Central Scots

The Central dialect of Scots stretches from West Angus and North-east Perthshire in the North, to Galloway and Ulster in the South West, and the River Tweed in the South East. Thus apart from the small Southern Scots area in the counties of Roxburgh, Selkirk, and East Dumfriesshire, Central Scots is spoken all over the Lowlands south and west of the Tay. It can be sub-divided into South Central, West Central, and East Central Scots – with the last showing differences north and south of the Forth – but the differences tend to be in accent rather than dialect. I can confirm that from personal experience. I was brought up in the West Central area but spent summer holidays in Fife, in the East Central area. The Fifers kidded me on about the elongated vowel sounds of Ayrshire Scots – 'Ye come fae near Kilmaaarnock!", and I imitated their singsong twang, but we spoke the same language. The difference was in accent. I recall an old worthy in Bowhill called Grace who used to visit my grandmother, acting as newsbearer and Greek chorus for the pit village. She invariably entered the house and with a suitably portentious pause, announced, "Ye kain Mrs Bruce that bides alang the road. . . well she's daid". In Ayrshire we would have said "ken" and "deid", but I always felt "daid" conveyed the mystery of death better than the stark finality of "deid".

With the medieval Scottish Court in session at Edinburgh, Linlithgow and Dunfermline the dialect of East Central Scotland is the nearest we can approach to imagining the Scots spoken by the likes of William Dunbar or James IV back in the language's Golden Age. North of the Forth the language retains its older forms with the area of West Angus or East Perthshire being more conservative in its retention of certain forms than Fife. For example, that area retains the older ae, ane, and aince, against the yae, yin, and yince of the other areas. Similarly the oo sound in mune, spune, and gude is retained in Angus, while to the south it has become muin, spuin, and guid, pronounced more or less as in Scottish Standard English bid. It was of course the spoken Scots of this area which proved such a rich source for Professor Lorimer when he began his mammoth translation of the New Testament into Scots; it has also proved to be a fertile source of poetry in the language with William Soutar, Violet Jacob and Helen B. Cruikshank just a few of the writers who hail from this heartland of Scots. The speech of the cities, of course, is farthest removed from the more classical rural dialects, but Perth and Dundee are still broadly Scots in speech, though the English accents of a "county set" can also be heard there. Dundee's unique feature is the eh sound for I, as in e.g. Eh hud meh eh on a peh – I had my eye on a pie. Theories such as the common one that it developed out of jute spinners having to mouth their words so that their fellow workers could lip-read above the clack of the mills are good stories, but little else. As in Glasgow, the local dialect of Scots was influenced by immigrants from further North in Scotland, but more especially by thousands of people from Ireland. Most of the latter came from Ulster, and you can hear a sound close to the eh in some parts of the North of Ireland. Edinburgh is Scotland's most anglicised city, at least in matters of speech. The reasons for this are many; the University, the high percentage of children who attend fee-paying schools, the old professional institutions such as the Law, whose members have changed considerably from Cockburn's day when they spoke Scots. The huge Edinburgh middle class tends to speak Standard English or Scottish Standard English. Scots is there too; a friend who was born and bred in the South Side speaks good Scots, so much so that people presume she is not a native of the city. Edinburgh is so dominated by the values of the middle classes, that working-class culture and speech has very low prestige even among the working class. In this I feel it differs substantially from it's rival in the West, Glasgow.

## West Central Scots

Whereas in Edinburgh the working class are defined by the predominant middle-class culture, in Glasgow the opposite prevails and the professional classes have some of the street wisdom and gallousness of the predominant working-class ethos of the city. The result of this is that almost everyone from Glasgow is recognisably Scottish in speech; in Edinburgh it is sometimes difficult to tell if someone is Scottish or English by their accent, in Glasgow that confusion rarely exists. The middle classes may not like the Glasgow dialect, but they are influenced by it. I recall my amusement when I lived in South Carolina and heard an old white gentleman apologise for the fact that their speech had been influenced by their close associations with the blacks. The inhabitants of Glasgow's West End are in a similar relationship to the speech of the masses. Glaswegian has enormous internal prestige. The strength of the dialect there lies with the strength of the working-class identity which is basic to people from the Western industrial belt. Also through the media working-class heroes such as footballers or comedians have given Glaswegian "underground" prestige in the rest of Scotland, so that it's influence is extending well beyond Glasgow – much to the horror of English and Scots purists alike. For both groups, Glaswegian expressions such as "a'm urnae gaun" and the plural "youz" are abhorrent shibboleths. The ultimate test of a dialect's worth is its ability to communicate, and there are few more extrovert communicators than Glaswegians. There are big differences between the speech of Glasgow and its Lanarkshire and Ayrshire hinterland, especially in the smaller industrial towns such as those in the Irvine Valley, and of course the country. Because most people with a West of Scotland accent live in Glasgow, Glaswegians are often surprised to hear Ayrshire people for example use Scots words and sounds which have been lost in the city dialect; ye ken for ye know, seiven for seven, brocht for brought etc. Other features of the Western dialect of Scots include the aw vowel giving snaw, baw, braw, whereas e.g. Angus would have snaa, baa, braa; the oo or ui vowel in do, muir, puir, teuch and eneuch are pronounced dae, mair, pair tyuch and inyuch; the Fife a vowel sound in parritch or bannet are pronounced purritch and bunnet in Ayrshire.

## South Central Scots

In South Ayrshire, West Dumfriesshire and Galloway you enter another subdivision of the Central or Mid Scots dialect area, South Central Scots. It retains a few more conservative features that have changed in North Ayrshire e.g. the words for tough and enough mentioned above still retain the older form of teuch and eneuch with the oo sound rather than the altered tyuch and inyuch of the West Central dialect. The West Central dialect appears though to be spreading into this area, and older people can point out the differences between the Scots of the older and the younger generations. Western Galloway has also long been influenced by communication with and settlement by Irish people. Wigtownshire is set apart for this reason by the neighbouring county of Kirkcudbright. There the people talk about going "over the Cree and into the

Irish" – the river marking the linguistic boundary. Ironically, though, some of the features people think of as Irish in Wigtownshire, are possibly older forms of Scots brought back to Scotland recently by the descendants of the Scots-speaking participants in the 17th-century Plantation of Ulster.

## Ulster Scots

Ulster Scots is derived from the West and South Central Scots of the thousands of Scots who emigrated to Ireland before and after James VI's Plantation of the province. As the only major contemporary Scots-speaking area outwith the borders of Scotland, it deserves more detailed consideration.

The official Plantation of Ulster in the reign of James VI took place only in the counties west of the River Bann. There English and Scottish "undertakers" settled with their countrymen on lands granted by the Crown. The result is an ethnic and linguistic patchwork which is still discernible; the localities which the Scots settled in East Donegal, Derry, and Tyrone are still Scots in speech. The Reverend John Graham of Maghera in County Londonderry described the situation as it pertained in the early 19th century.

> In reporting the language and customs peculiar to this neighbourhood, attention must be paid to the usual division of the inhabitants into English, Irish and Scotch. The dialect and customs of these distinct races are as different from each other as their respective creeds. . . The Dissenters speak broad Scotch, and are in the habit of using terms and expressions long since obsolete, even in Scotland, and which are only to be found in the glossary annexed to the bishop of Dunkeld's translation of Virgil

The reference to the poetry of Gavin Douglas is apt, not only because Ulster Scots, being more remote from the anglicising influences sweeping Scotland, preserves older forms of the language, but also because the Scots "ower the sheugh" as they call it continued to have a passion for literature in Scots. But whereas Scots settlement West of the Bann is interspersed with English and Irish communities, Antrim, North Down and the Ards peninsula are almost entirely Scots in culture and language, with the native Irish community speaking a form of Ulster Scots as well. When Irish-speaking seasonal labourers travelled from West Donegal to help in the harvest in the rich farmlands of lowland Ulster, they made reference to "lifting the Scotch" – picking up the language of the farmers. These areas of East Ulster began to be settled before the official Plantation, and continued to attract immigrants from Scotland long after the Plantation scheme had ended.

Inspired by the success of Burns, the area produced a prolific Scots poetic tradition, particularly among the hand-loom weavers; the same men were in the vanguard of the United Irishmen and their efforts to create Home Rule for Ireland. Then Presbyterian Dissenters and Catholics were united in the same cause. When the movement was quelled, many left Ulster for the religious freedom of America – the "Scotch Irish" as they are called there forming 15% of the population at the turn of the 19th century. James Orr of Ballycarry, Co. Antrim described their departure in 'The Passengers'.

> How calm an' cozie is the wight,
> Frae cares an' conflicts clear ay,
> Whase settled headpiece never made,
> His heels or han's be weary!
> Perplex'd is he whase anxious schemes
> Pursue applause, or siller,
> Success nor sates, nor failure tames;
> Bandied frae post to pillar.
> Is he, ilk day.
>
> As we were, Comrades, at the time
> We mov't frae Ballycarry,
> To wan'er thro' the woody clime
> Burgoyne gied oure to harrie:
> Wi' frien's consent we prie't a gill,
> An' monie a house did call at,
> Shook han's, an' smil't; tho ilk fareweel
> Strak, like a weighty mallet,
> Our hearts, that day.

That stanza form of course is very prevalent in Scots verse and is used by both Fergusson in 'Leith Races' and Burns in 'The Holy Fair'. The weaver poets were aware of the tradition to which they belonged, and proud of it as an expression of community. Hugh Porter of Down writes.

> . . . And thirdly, in the style appears

> The accent o' my earlier years
> Which is not Scotch, nor English either,
> But part o' baith mixed up thegither.
> Yet it's the sort my neighbours use,
> Wha think 'shoon' prettier far than 'shoes'.

Since the days of the United Irishmen, the pressures against Ulster Scots have been similar to those against Scots in Scotland, with the dialects there classified as "provincial and barbaric". That the professional classes were adopting Standard English and creating a division between themselves and the common people is revealed in James Orr's poem 'The Irish Cottier's', which is based on Burns' 'The Cottar's Saturday Night'. Here the local minister visits the home of a dying cottar.

> The minister comes in, wha' to the poor,
> Without a fee performs the doctor's part:
> An' while wi' hope he soothes the suff'rer's heart,
> An' gies a cheap, safe recipe, they try
> To quat braid Scotch, a task that foils their art;
> For while they join his converse, vain though shy,
> They monie a lang learn'd word misca' an' misapply.

Today though the dialect is still spoken strongly, especially in Antrim and the Ards, and the tradition of writing folk poetry in it prevails, as Alex McAllister from Larne humorously demonstrated in 'The Mother Tongue'. It suffers from the same lack of status as in Scotland, and like here, the prevailing feeling is that it is dying. Like here though, it has a long time to go yet. The following extract from 'The Humours of Druids Island' by Archibald McIlroy, gives the flavour of the Antrim dialect at the turn of the century. It concerns some ladies gathering for tea.

> No yin o' the ithers had the guid manners tae tak' aff their gloves, which made it very awkward for me, – for on account of my rheumatics, a wear knitted wool gloves a' the year roon. A didna daur tak' them aff, an' no a haet could a dae wi them on; for while a was fummlin an tryin tae get a haud o the wee bit cup han'le the half o the tay got jebbled intae the saucer. The slice o' breid fell in pieces in my lap; for a couldna bring mysel' tae rowl it up like a lettuce as the ithers were daein', havin' always been teach't that it's the worst o' manners tae dooble up yer piece; an a was that much put aboot that a

could nether eat nor drink; so a slipped oot my han'kerchie',
gathered up the breid in't an stuffed it in my pocket; an what
was left o the tay a emp'ied intae a floerpot that was sittin'
on the table; an dae ye know, they wur a' that busy gossipin'
intae ithers lugs that no yin o' them saw me.

## Southern Scots

Southern Scots or Border Scots as it is sometimes called is the
dialect spoken in the counties of Roxburgh, Selkirk and East
Dumfriesshire. Apart from a stretch of land between Carlisle
and Gretna where Scots and the Cumbrian dialect mix and
merge – a linguistic parallel to the old "Debatable Grund"
between the two kingdoms – the dialects spoken on either side
of the Border are markedly different. The *Scottish National
Dictionary* affirms this: 'For all practical purposes the political
and linguistic boundaries may be considered to coincide.'

The most noticeable feature of this dialect to Scots-speakers
from other areas is the lack of what we think of as the
characteristically Scots sounds of oo in doon, coo and broon,
or ee in wee, bree or gie, and their replacement with the
diphthongs ow and ey, which sound English to us. For this
reason it is often known as the 'yow an mey' dialect, a feature
emphasised by local rhymes.

Yow an' meyee, an the bern dor keyee,
The sow an' the threyee weyee pigs.

Yow an mey'll gang out an pow a pey
(you and me will go out and pull a pee)

Diphthongs are fairly rare in Scots, so the prevalence of them
within a rich dialect of Scots strikes the outsider as unusual.
Another vowel which is diphthongised is the ai sound in baith,
braid and claes, which here becomes something like beeath,
breead, and cleeaz. Another feature of the dialect which
closely ressembles English is their use of a vowel sound close
to the southern Standard English back, bad and bat. Other
dialect speakers used to send up the Borderers 'posh' accent
by pronouncing Nellie as Nallie, bed as bad, and pen as pan.
The people who speak "the saft lawland tongue o the Border"
take all this in their stride; pushed up against the Border they
have an intense national pride in their Scottishness, an identity

enhanced by being tied in with the fierce local loyalties you can feel in ancient burghs like Selkirk, and not only at Common Riding time. Walter Elliot of Selkirk writes articles on Border Scots in the *Southern Reporter*, and also publishes local poetry in Scots. The poem that begins 'The clash-ma-clavers Chap Book' makes wry comment on the change over from Scots to English in his native Ettrick.

Ah only sterted writin
Tae preserve ma mither tongue
An the language that was spoken
In the days when Ah was young.

Noo there's fewer folk in Ettrick,
It's maistly aa wee trees
An Dykers are ootnumbered
Bie Liberal M.P.'s.

Then there's the Ettrick English
(An they're really aa nice folk)
Bit they didnae ken oor faithers
Or the language that they spoke.

Ah hope ye'll like the efforts
In this wee book o rhyme
The verse is often rotten
Bit the language is sublime

Much of the beautiful Border country has been settled by retired people from England, another phenomenon affecting the linguistic balance in the region. The Borderers tend to "gang thegither" when their culture is threatened, and their innate thrawnness makes them hold on to their Scots, and no be blate to use it in every social circumstance. They are aware that the Border Ballads are among the finest composed in any language; the language happens to be Border Scots, and they see no reason why they should give it up. Another unique feature of Southern Scots is the large number of words which have entered the Scots of the area from the Romany language of the gypsies whose headquarters were always associated with Yetholm in Roxburghshire. Words like barry, meaning good, or radge meaning enraged or excited, spread into the mixed Scots/English speech of Berwick nearby, and recently have become part of the colloquial vocabulary of urban teenagers.

This verse by Thomas Grey published in the *Berwick Advertiser* in 1910, gives a flavour of the Romany words.

> A "Gadgie" when he is a "Chor"
> A "Jugal" always fears,
> For "Jugals" as a rule are kept
> By "Gadgies" with big "keirs".

(*gadgie* man; *chor* thief; *jugal* dog; *keir* house).

Although the characteristics mentioned make this dialect unique, it is still one which in intonation and pronunciation is not unlike the Central Scots dialects lying to the east, west and north to West Angus and Perthshire. It is only there, north-east of Dundee, that we enter the dialects of Northern Scots, which are so different and distinctive from Central Scots, that some regard for example the Buchan dialect almost as a separate language; it is not, and once the lugs have adjusted to the radically different intonation, pronunciation and sounds of these dialects, you soon realise that they are simply beautiful richly textured dialects of the same language as is spoken in the south of the country.

## Northern Scots

Northern Scots stretches from East Angus and the Mearns in the south to Caithness in the north, and includes the great bulge of fertile land between the Moray Firth and the North Sea known as the North-East, an area which has strong claims to be the heartland of spoken Scots in our day.

Coastal Angus and the Mearns appear to be a transitional area from Central Scots to North-East Scots. It has some, but not all of the distinguishing features of the North-East. Here as further North, Central Scots aw in braw and baw becomes braa and baa; bane and stane becomes been and steen; wha and whit becomes fa and fit. But once you are north of Stonehaven and beyond the Dee, the sound changes from Central Scots become more numerous and distinctive. While the Mearns has the f sound only in the words who, where, what, and when, in Aberdeenshire and Buchan the f replaces wh in almost every instance; whistle and whippet become fussle and fuppet. Central Scots and North-East differ radically in their vowel sounds; muin and spuin become meen and

speen; guid and schuil become gweed and skweel; the vowel
in bide, mine or wei is pronounced almost like the oy in boy
– Central Scots "whit wei?" becoming North-East "fit woi?";
Central Scots wame becomes wyme and the ee sound in speik
or sweit becomes spyke and swyte; naikit and caird become
nyakit and cyard. In the Buchan dialect there are consonant
changes as well; faither, mither and brither become fader,
midder and bridder; wrocht and wricht becomes vrocht and
vricht; the unsounded k in knie or knock is sounded in the
North-East, as it is in German. This is a sound that is dying
out of the dialect now. Similarly the gn of gnaw used to be
sounded, and is still sounded in the word gnap; gnappin or
gneppin is the derogatory term people in the Northern Scots
area use for folk who affect English, or talk posh. The strength
and vitality of Scots in the area is such that even those who
"gnap" take an interest in their "Doric" as an expression of the
strong regional identity.

   That identity has been seen by outsiders as a parochial one,
and sent up in apocryphal stories such as the mythical (I hope)
headline in the *Aberdeen Press and Journal* – "NORTH EAST
MAN DROWNED" with in smaller letters beneath, "Titanic
sinks". The identity is undoubtedly a source of the strength
of traditional Scots culture in the area, and other regions of
Scotland could be doing with a bit of it. But it is an identity
produced by very different social circumstances from those
which pertained in, for example, the Central Lowlands. There
industrialisation and the resultant influx of immigrants changed
the local language and culture dramatically. In the North-
East, farming and fishing were the mainstays of the economy
until very recently – activities which encouraged local culture
and speech to thrive isolated from outside influences. Indeed,
the North-East is a series of local cultures and dialects rather
than a monolithic homogeneous one. The fishing communities
traditionally were cut off from the farming hinterland, and you
can hear the result of that in the local variations of the dialect.
Lossiemouth and Hopeman on the Morayshire coast differ
from each other considerably, but they share features which
do not prevail in the rural dialects inland. Again Hopeman
is different from Burghead a mile or so along the coast; the
linguistic line separating Scots and Highland English appears
to pass between the towns, creating markedly different ways of

speaking in the two communities. Moray and Nairn generally differ from the rest of the North-East area in that they do not have the North-East meer or peer sound, but the more common Scots muir or puir.

The self-contained nature and comparative isolation of the fisher and farming communities meant that the Scots of the region is conservative and "old-fashioned", preserving a wealth of vocabulary which has been lost in other areas. The spoken dialects are strong, and it is just as well; the rapid social change in the area precipitated by the discovery of oil is producing the kind of challenge to the local culture posed by industrialisation to the south of the country in the late 18th and early 19th centuries. The romantic image of rangy chieldes like Long Rob and Chae in *Sunset Song* speaking pure Buchan Doric in a remote Howe somewhere north of Alford, I am afraid is becoming less and less based on reality. When I made enquiries in Aberdeenshire for a primary school in the Buchan heartland, I found that every school I contacted the same situation prevailed; a high percentage of the children came from English, American or West of Scotland backgrounds, so it was practically impossible to find a place where the native children spoke an unadulterated form of the dialect. Clatt, where I filmed and recorded schoolchildren, the local primary teacher, and a farmer called Duncan Muirden (whose beautiful use of Scots could have graced the pages of Gibbon's novel) was chosen for its distance from the city and from the effects of oil, but the situation was the same there as elsewhere. The positive sign of the cultural mixture that is going on there, is that Scots seems to be holding its own.

The incoming children are picking up the local dialect, and like the locals, becoming bilingual. Helping this to happen is the fact that Scots poetry seems to be taught more in the North-East than elsewhere, and is given some status by the regional education authorities; one Director of Education recently edited an impressive collection of Scots verse titled *Ten North East Poets* which is widely used in the region. From Alexander Ross at the end of the 18th century through till the present day, the North-East has been the most vital area in regional literature in Scots, with poets like David Rorie, Charles Murray, J.C. Milne, and Flora Garry contributing important work. This is an example, Flora Garry's poem, 'Bennygoak'.

It was jist a skelp of the muckle furth,
A skylter o roch grun,
Fin grandfadder's fadder bruke it in
Fae the hedder an the funn.
Granfadder sklatit barn an byre,
Brocht water to the closs,
Pat fail-dykes ben the bare brae face
An a cairt road tull the moss.

Bit wir fadder sottert i the yard
An skeppit amo' bees
An keepit fancy dyeuks an doos
'at warna muckle eese.
He bocht aul' wizzent horse an kye
An scrimpit muck an seed;
Syne, clocherin wi a craichly hoast,
He dwine't awa, an deed.

I look far ower by Ythanside
To Fyvie's laich, lythe lan's,
To Auchterless an Bennachie
An the mist-blue Grampians.
Sair't o the hull o Bennygoak
An scunnert o the ferm,
Gin I bit daar't, gin I bit daar't,
I'd flit the comin' term.

(*funn* whin; *closs* farmyard; *fail dyke* sod wall; *skeppit amo'
bees* kept bees; *sottert* idled; *dyeuks an doos* ducks and doves;
*clocherin..hoast* wheezing cough; *dwine* fade; *laich* low)

One of the highlights of my visit to Clatt was to hear two wee
girls from the South East of England recite J.K. Annand's poem
'The Crocodile' in Buchan Scots. Many of the children there
of course live on farms – and there is no danger of the dialect
disappearing as long as it remains relevant to the way of life.
The test, I suppose is whether North-East Scots can adapt to
the new economy of the area. The fact that Aberdeen city is
still in general healthily Scots in speech is a sign that it will.
Outsiders smile when Aberdeen shop assistants say "Hae a braa
day" – the translation of the ubiquitous Americanism "Have a
nice day", but it is nevertheless a sign of adaptation to outside
influence, rather than a renunciation of the local language. More
than any other Scottish city, Aberdeen maintains close personal
and cultural ties to its hinterland, and its language and culture.
That is another reason why North-East literature enjoys such

popularity and credence within education, for there is little of the notion of two cultures – the urban v. rural conflict which bedevils attitudes to Scots in Glasgow for example. For the literature of the North-East, like the traditional music, tends to be about the muckle fermtouns or the crofts of the area. It is very much a dialect literature, with the spellings often reflecting local forms, rather than following the more classical spelling conventions of literary Scots. As with literature in the Glasgow or Shetland dialect, this makes it more difficult for outsiders to read, but has the benefit of being immediate and intimate for those who speak the dialect as their mither tongue. This is how William Alexander opens his novel *Johnny Gibb of Gushetneuk*; the orra loon Tam Meerison is helping Johnny to yoke the cairt. As with the Burns letter earlier, ye'll hae tae consult the dictionary for the vocabulary.

"Heely, heely, Tam, ye glaiket stirk – ye hinna on the hin shelvin' o' the cairt. Fat hae ye been haiverin at, min? That cauf saick'll be tint owre the back door afore we win a mile fae hame, See't yer belly-ban' be ticht aneuch noo. Woo, lassie! man, ye been makin' a hantle mair adee aboot blaikin that graith o' yours, an' kaimin the mear's tail, nor balancin' yer cairt, an' gettin' the things packit in till't."

"Sang, that's nae vera easy deen, I can tell ye, wi' sic a mengyie o' them. Faur'll aw pit the puckle girss to the mear?"

"Ou, fat's the eese o' that lang stoups ahin, aw wud like tae ken? Lay that bit bauk across, an' syne tak' the aul' pleuch ryn there, an' wup it ticht atween the stays; we canna hae the beast's maet trachel't amo' their feet. Foo muckle corn pat ye in?"

"Four lippies –gweed–mizzour–will that dee?"

"We'se lat it be deein. Is their trock a' in noo, I won'er?"

"Nyod, seerly it is."

The last branch of Northern Scots is spoken in a few coastal settlements in Inverness-shire, Easter Ross and Sutherland, and more substantially in the populous lowland east of Caithness. Caithness apart, this area has been Gaelic-speaking until comparatively recently in its linguistic history; when Gaelic has waned it has tended to be replaced with Highland English rather than Scots. Communities like Avoch in the Black Isle however have been Scot-speaking "plantations" in the Gaidhealtachd since the 17th century; surrounded by Gaelic and separated from other Scots-speaking communities until recently, Avoch preserves older forms of Scots which have died out elsewhere, and which appear "foreign" to other Scots speakers. These examples of the Avoch dialect from the *Scottish National Dictionary* illustrate the point well; "Twuz a braa knap o' a sheelie an' no a dymock" – it was a fine knap of a boy and not a girl. "Al keyme thee dossan for thee" – I'll comb your hair for you".

The Black Isle and Caithness dialects share the same features which distinguish this dialect area from the North-East. The diphthong ow is common e.g. dowg for dog, cowld for cold, bowld for bold. These remind one of Irish English; curiously the same sound occurs in Kintyre, a similar Scots-speaking island surrounded by a sea of Gaelic. It is possibly a Gaelic influence on the speech, for the Caithness dialect includes many Gaelic as well as Norse words in its vocabulary. Other noticeable features in the speech of people from Caithness is the use of sh for ch, making cheese and chimney in the dialect sheeze and shumley; and the replacement of the initial j sound in judge and jury with ch, giving chudge and chury. The th at the beginning of the, that, they, there etc. is dropped giving ee, at, ey, and ere – for example "Fas at 'ere?" – "Who's that there?" Often in Caithness dialect, in the, on the, at the, of the, are reduced to the sound 'e giving e.g. "He bides 'e centre 'e toon" – He lives in the centre of the town. Caithness and Sutherland were at one time part of the Norse sphere of influence, and the John o' Groats area is particularly close to Orkney in speech. The Scandinavian linguistic heritage is even more clearly evident in the dialects of Orkney and Shetland.

## Insular Scots

The dialects of the Northern Isles differ from the Scots of mainland Scotland in the more recent and more profound influence that the Norse language exercised here. Scots already has a strong Scandinavian legacy; to flit, to big (build), loof (palm) and nieve (fist) are just a few everyday examples in the language. Some of these words have been in Scots since the settlers from the English Danelaw established themselves in the new burghs in the 11th century. In Orkney and Shetland, however the Norse influence was much more direct, because of the Norse occupation of these islands from the 8th to the 15th century. The islands were transferred from Danish to

Scottish jurisdiction in 1468. Only then did the Scandinavian language of the islands, Norn, come into constant contact with Scots. Through the political power enjoyed by the Scots, the Norn language was gradually eroded and replaced by Scots over the following centuries. There was a period of bilingualism; in 1680 a minister reported of the people of Cunningsburgh in Shetland: "[they] seldom speak other [than Norn] among themselves, yet all of them speak the Scots tongue more promptly and more properly than generally they do in Scotland." The similarities between Scots and Norn, and the number of shared words facilitated the transition from Norn to Scots. . . as it facilitated the transition from Scots to English more recently. Dr Marwick, in the introduction to his book *The Orkney Norn*, states: "..before it ultimately died, the Norn tongue must have been increasingly impregnated with words from Scots. Yet the change was something more than a steady inflation of Norn with Scots words, until it became more Scots than Norn. What probably happened was that the common everyday phraseology of Norn ceased and was replaced by the corresponding Scots terms of speech."

Although Scots and eventually English replaced Norn, there remained many words from the older language which continued in everyday use by the people of the islands. When the Faeroese scholar Jakob Jakobsen researched the Norn influence on the Shetland dialect at the end of the 19th century, he found that 10,000 words of Norn origin were still extant, though half of them were only remembered by older folk. Many of the words were intimately bound to the local way of life, and the sensitivity to the natural environment required by fishermen and crofters; pirr, laar, flan, bat, gouster, vaelensi are different strengths and kinds of wind. Some of these words are still in common use, though in the introduction to *The Shetland Dictionary*, John G Graham points out that of the 720 words beginning h in Jakobsen's dictionary, approximately 65 could be identified by a young Shetlander today. The dialects of the Northern Isles also preserve older forms of Scots and vocabulary like owsen, thrawart, or grice which have disappeared from most mainland dialects. Because of the isolated nature of the many island communities in both Orkney and Shetland, there are many locally distinct features in the various dialects. The following are a few of the more general features of Insular Scots.

Voiced th is replaced by d, so the becomes da; thy, thee and thine are all still current in Shetland, pronounced dy, dee, dine as in the following example from the *Shetland Dictionary*: "I hoop dy bairn is as god ta dee is my ane has bon ta me". The unvoiced th in for example thin, thick or thrapple becomes tin, tick or trapple. The personal pronoun has two forms "du" and "you" used like the French tu and vous. A Shetland girl I once knew used to greet mc with thc delightful, "Foo is du, my chewel?", which is almost as nice in English, "How are you, my jewel?" The auxiliary verb to be is used in places where English has to have; instead of "I have written", "I'm written" would be used. The Shetland dialect in particular has undergone a revival of interest in recent years; the threat to the way of life posed by the oil industry has galvanised the people into action for their culture, and a more enlightened attitude exists in the local radio station and the local Education Authority to the dialect than that which prevails in most parts of Scotland. The dialect's prestige is also helped with the growth of a strong dialect literature, which has modern exponents like Rhoda Bulter. One of the most famous Shetland poems is 'Aald Maunsie's Cro' by Basil Anderson; the end of Maunsie ends my chapter on the dialects of Scots, and provides an example of Shetland poetry.

> Time booed his rigg and shore his tap
> An laid his cro in mony a slap;
> Snug-shorded by his ain hert-steyn
> He lost his senses een by een,
> Till lyin helpless laek a paet
> Nor kail nor mutton he could aet,
> Sae deed, as what we au maun do,
> Hae we or hae we no a cro.

(*cro* an enclosure for growing cabbages; *booed his rigg* bowed his backbone; *shore his tap* sheared his top; *slap* ditch; *shorded* propped, supported; *hert steyn* hearthstone)

# Chapter 11

## The Future Oors?

For most Scottish people, feelings about their native culture are fraught with powerful dichotomies which pull individuals in different directions. Pride and prejudice, love and hatred, reverence and contempt – Scots tend to react with extremes of feeling to different aspects of their culture. You may well say that is the right of the individual in every free nation, and I would agree. But the extreme reactions in Scotland are a direct result of the lack of Scottish content in the educational system and to a lesser extent, the shortage of it in the all-pervasive media which helps form ideas in the second part of the 20th century. When Scottish history or literature is not taught, the implication for many is that it is not worth teaching. Many in fact draw the conclusion that it does not exist. With no grounding in their culture, objective assessment of its worth is well-nigh impossible and frequently people react with a passion which astonishes outsiders. The frequent eruption of letters discussing the minutiae of Scottish speech in the *Glasgow Herald* and the *Scotsman*, for example, and the intensity of the debate provoked is apparently a uniquely Scottish phenomenon.

This passion for things Scottish is often an instinctive gut reaction to the culture being put down by the authorities, the reaction against it often the product of derived irrational prejudice. Like Pavlov's dogs many Scots are conditioned to react to any aspect of their culture with the word "parochial" or "tartan" or "couthy", no matter how universal the content may be. One of the few unfavourable reviews of 'The Mother Tongue' series on television appeared in the *Glasgow Herald*'s Last Night's View column. There Helen Graham stated that "every couthy word" I said had her "jumping up and down with rage". Now in an attempt to fit 14 centuries of linguistic history into three half-hour programmes, there was no room for couthy reminiscence, and the extracts from the literature, the vigorous dialects represented, and the top writers and academics who contributed again expressed a vision that was far from couthy. Yet hers is a standard reaction, as typical as any other. Lacking the objectivity education in the culture would give, the typical Scottish reaction is intensely personal rather than considered and objective. George Gordon, Lord Byron's autobiographical lines in the poem 'Don Juan' sum up the dichotomy perfectly:

> But I am half a Scot by birth, and bred
> A whole one, and my heart flies to my head.

Being educated as an Englishman, yet having folk-pride in being Scottish without knowing exactly why you should be proud, is again a typical Scottish experience and has interesting social consequences. Every Scot will assert that he belongs to a nation rather than a region or a province. Ask the same person however whether the national history, literature and language should be an integral part of the educational system and you will get a very different, possibly uncomfortable response. For this type of question demands a lot more of the person's Scottishness than supporting the fitba team, and most have not had the training to help formulate a considered reply.

At the core of all this is the complex question of language. It is a veritable tinder box of a subject, for although only a tiny group of people have had the opportunity to study it, everyone has very strong opinions on the matter. This is not surprising, as language is central to people's being and as I have shown Scotland has long been a linguistic battlefield. For many folk the local dialect of Scots is literally the Mither Tongue, and is held dear as an integral part of their identity, even though they are conditioned to speak it only in certain social situations. The heart and head division among native speakers of Scots is beautifully expressed by Lewis Grassic Gibbon in this passage from *Sunset Song*.

> So that was Chris and her reading and schooling, two Chrisses there were that fought for her heart and tormented her. You hated the land and the coarse speak of the folk and learning was brave and fine one day and the next you'd waken with the peewits crying across the hills, deep and deep, crying in the heart of you and the smell of the earth in your face, almost you'd cry for that, the beauty of it and the sweetness of the

Scottish land and skies. You saw their faces in firelight, father's and mother's and the neighbours', before the lamps lit up, tired and kind, faces dear and close to you, you wanted the words they'd known and used, forgotten in the far-off youngness of their lives, Scots words to tell to your heart, how they wrung it and held it, the toil of their days and unendingly their fight. And the next minute that passed from you, you were English, back to the English words so sharp and clean and true – for a while, for a while, till they slid so smooth from your throat you knew they could never say anything that was worth the saying at all.

If a little sentimental and very much based on the rural experience, passages like that were powerful enough to hook this fifteen-year-old town dweller on literature when he was given the book as a school prize. It was the first time I realised that literature could be about me and mine and the effect had the force of revelation. Gibbon's depiction of the Scots/English dichotomy of language fitted my own experience perfectly, and made me understand it better. Yet many make, I feel, false divisions between town and country speech, making evaluations based on class prejudice rather than linguistic truth. The "peasant" of the country is regarded by the middle classes as an admirable character, while the "keelie" of the city working class is despicable. It is a fallacy which goes back to the Romantic Age; the German folklorist Herder encapsulated the belief in this statement about the urban masses: "The mob in the streets which never sings or composes but shrieks and mutilates, is not the people". I have had a few backhanders in print myself, because of this prejudice. The television page of the Glasgow *Evening Times* printed beneath the billing for an Odyssey programme the words – "Billy Kay, the man with the broadest accent in broadcasting, mouths gutteral [sic] noises about the Temperance Movement". They did however have the courage to publish my reply which suggested that they were not only insulting me but 90% of their readers who make the same "guttural noises".

Tragically the urban versus rural division is a live and divisive issue among those who actually know something about the history of Scots and frequently use it to excellent effect in poetry and prose. Many Glasgow writers have nothing to do with Scots and relegate it as the irrelevant dialect of an idealised rural past. Its advocates are regarded as retrogressive nationalists. Much of this however is a perhaps understandable reaction against the dismissal of the Glasgow dialect by both English and Scots linguistic purists. Fuelling the controversy is the unfortunate remark made in the introduction of the *Scottish National Dictionary*: "Owing to the influx of Irish and foreign immigrants in the industrial area near Glasgow the dialect has become hopelessly corrupt". The disenfranchisement of the huge immigrant population which is now completely Scottish in culture is implicit in that statement and is naturally a source of resentment. However the Lallans purists who dismiss urban speech as corrupt Scots and the urban writers who in turn dismiss Scots as an irrelevancy to modern industrial society are both equally off the mark. Scots is spoken in the cities and the urban dialects are every bit as vigorous and racy as the rural ones. Scots is also the language of people who live in towns and work in mines and mills, a language of gutsy realism and focus for a life style quite removed from the rural idyll. Scots is also the language of the ethnic groups who have added their distinctive contribution to Scottish society. The immigrants learned the language of the people and the people's language was and is a form of Scots. I was never able to record the Scots/Yiddish dialect of the Jewish commercial travellers recalled lovingly by David Daiches in his autobiography, *Two Worlds, an Edinburgh Jewish childhood* where a common barmitzvah saying was "wull ye hae a drap o the bramfen" – the Yiddish for whisky! I have however recorded for Odyssey the rich mell of Scots spoken by first-generation Lithuanians, Italians and Spaniards in different parts of Scotland. The last group settled in the iron and coal area of Logan, near Cumnock in South Ayrshire. I remember beginning an interview with an old man born in Seville, both of us speaking our Ayrshire Scots. Shortly in to the interview, however, Mr Esquierdo gradually switched to English and would have continued in the same had his wife not intervened, "Talk Scoatch you, stoap pittin it oan". She too was born in Spain, but like the people around her had absorbed Scots as the language closest to her adopted community – a source of identity for her and her family.

The artificial divisions that have arisen between Scots purists on the one side and Glasgow writers on the other is one in which reaction against what one side has said prevails over logic. Entrenched positions have been established which are untenable because there are no hard-and-fast rules in language – it is fluid, flexible and ever-changing. Besides, the pressures against local speech forms are exactly the same in rural Buchan and urban Glasgow, and it is time the different factions realised this and called for acceptance of all speech forms indigenous to the country. To do that a national focus will be a lot more powerful than a local one based on the Doric or Glaswegian.

One of the fundamental problems facing the continuation of Scots and all the facets of Scottish culture which make the country distinctive and unique is the conflict between regional and national identities within Scotland, and the country's definition as a region in the rest of the U.K. The desire to encourage Scottish culture often runs up against the fear of upsetting the monolithic British status quo whose values the majority of Scots are conditioned to adhere to. J Derrick McClure examines the phenomenon in detail in *Chapman* 41, where he quotes the following responses from teachers asked to consider the feasibility and desirability of expanding Scottish studies in the schools and introducing a separate S.E.D. paper on Scottish Literature and Language.

> Scottish studies have a place in education, but I'm suspicious of the intentions behind the movement. All children should be encouraged to take an interest in their cultural heritage as a means of aiding the discovery of their own identity, both local and national – this, however, shouldn't simply become a means of instilling political values.

> Where do we draw the line in defining national heritage? The implications may be too far-reaching, especially in the political sense.

Now there is nothing inherently political in wanting to teach a country's heritage – that should be the natural birthright of all mankind. But Scots culture has been suppressed or remained on the periphery for so long that the thought of giving it status provokes feelings of unease and insecurity. This reaction is provoked both by guilt feelings about ignorance of things Scottish and fear of the responsibility of having to teach them on the part of teachers who have not themselves been educated in the subject. Fear of political implications – claymores under the bed, the dismissal of Scots literature as "difficult" or "parochial" or "not as good as Shakespeare" are all expressions of the same syndrome: the conflict between the national and the provincial in the Scottish mentality. Fionn MacColla went to the root of the conflict in his book *At the Sign of the Clenched Fist*: "Scottish education regards itself as successful, as having fulfilled its objective, in proportion as each generation is less Scottish than the last, in language, knowledge, culture, and consciousness". The situation has improved in recent decades but MacColla's statement rings true to the experience of most Scots alive today. The Portuguese colonies in Africa gave the name "assimilado" to the members of the native population who adopted not only the language and the culture of Portugal but also the Portuguese contempt for the native culture. To some extent Scotland is a country of assimilados, with everyone educated here inheriting this ambivalence about the Scottish/English balance within themselves and their culture. Some refer to it as the Scottish Cringe and it affects every individual and every institution to a greater or lesser extent. BBC Scotland for example is defined within the Corporation as a "National Region" and is constantly trying to work out whether it is "regional" or "national" and quite often finds it difficult to ride both horses at once. Gains have been made in recent years and Radio Scotland, after a disastrous start, is beginning to live up to its claim to be Scotland's National Network, offering a wide range of programmes with a definite Scottish voice and perspective. The BBC charter states that its aim is to reflect the distinctive features of Scottish culture. A sign of it having achieved that goal will be when Scots along with Scottish English is accepted as a natural medium of communication. That the Odyssey series, with its rich mell of different Scots dialects, was broadcast on Radio 4 U.K. is also a sign that there is greater acceptance of undiluted Scottish material in radio than television. In television, ratings often determine the purse strings, and that works against reflecting the "minority" culture of five million Scots. There is great resistance to Scottish programmes in London, and programme makers here know that they will only make the network if they make programmes that have no strong Scottish cultural base. Fortunately, that has not stopped them making good Scottish programmes for the few Scottish slots in the schedules. But as money gets tighter, there is a danger that the Scottish option will be chosen even less than before. Drama apart, Scotland's major representatives on the screens of Britain will continue to be Beethoven and Brahms! Even if you accept that Scottish culture is regional, surely by population alone that regional culture and its distinctive "dialect", music and literature should have a far greater presence on British Television.

Many people believe that the tension can only be resolved when Scotland achieves the political autonomy she has been requesting politely since the days of Keir Hardie. Only then will Scottish culture be central to our education, our media and our life. That may well be true, because it will take a giant admission of wrong on the part of the Scottish Establishment to alter the position radically. Establishments rarely admit that the central thrust of an age-old policy is wrong! Political change may be necessary, but it should not be. The case for Scottish language and the culture it has expressed is watertight by whatever cultural criterion you care to draw upon, be it in a Scottish, British, European, or world context. For us Scots, the language is fundamental to our present identity and essential to an understanding of our history and literary tradition. We are heir to this tradition and our linguistic and psychological inheritance make us more sensitive to its genius than other people. It is our duty to our children's children to ensure that Scots never becomes an alien tongue or they will be strangers to the traditions that have nurtured us and give us a unique place in the world. In that world there are over twenty-five million people of Scots descent. We are guardians of their tradition as well. The survival and revival of Scots is of vital importance to British and European culture – an integral and vivid part of the multicultured tapestry of European life. Provençal and Scots were the mediums of Europe's greatest literature at different periods of the Middle Ages, so knowledge of the language is essential for recall of important phases in European life. The greatest literature written in Britain between Chaucer and Spencer was produced in Scots by the makars. When the English break out of their phillistinely parochial and debilitating attitude of superiority towards the other cultures of Britain, they will recognise the brilliant alternative and complement to their own glittering literary tradition, here on their very doorstep. Scottish culture is important nationally and internationally. The irony or tragedy of its lack of status in its homeland is one that only fully strikes home when it is seen in a world context. In the "new" countries of the English-speaking world, American, Canadian and Australian literature are taught as a matter of course at school and university. In the American South, a part of the world whose landscape I know well and whose literature was practically derived from Walter Scott, Southern literature is naturally taught in all her universities. In Scotland, whose literature goes back centuries before any of these countries and is in most cases superior to them, there is only one department of Scottish literature in a Scottish University and pupils can actually go through the whole of the Scottish educational system without reading a single Scottish novel. When you try to explain as best you can to intelligent foreigners why this is the case, you still meet with astonished incomprehension. It is impossible for any civilised being to comprehend why one of the oldest and richest literatures in Europe is not taught in its native country. We Scots are so used to the situation that most of us are unconscious that an anomaly exists. Foreign scholars, however, who specialise in Scottish literature are extremely aware of the culture's lack of prestige in its homeland.

In 1984 the Fourth International Conference on Scottish Language and Literature – Medieval and Renaissance was held at the Scottish Studies Centre in the Germersheim Campus of the University of Mainz in West Germany. Here is part of an open letter, sometimes known as the Germersheim Declaration, signed by distinguished scholars from all over the world.

> The undersigned members of the Germersheim conference believe that young Scots deserve to have far more opportunity than they are now given to learn about the history and present situation of the native languages of Scotland and to acquire some understanding of their own patterns of speech and tolerance for those of other members of the Scottish community. We believe that the Scottish Education Department and other educational bodies should now take positive action to this end, and also that the press and the broadcasting media should now seriously consider whether their treatment and exposure of native varieties of Scots is fair and adequate; we ourselves believe it falls far short of this. It is particularly important that the potential of Scots as a means of communication in Scotland beyond the conveying of the humorous, the sentimental, the nostalgic and the trivial should be actively developed. This potential is amply

illustrated by 600 years of distinguished literature in Scots, access to which is the right of every Scot.

One of the stock Scottish media replies to such statements is that you cannot broadcast Braid Buchan, for example, because people in Glasgow will not understand it. It is the classic Catch 22 situation, and many Scots broadcasters have renegued on their responsibility and used this as an excuse not to broadcast the dialect. If they had gone ahead and allowed the native language on the airwaves, Braid Buchan would be as easily grasped by the Glaswegian as the dialects of Dallas, Lancashire, or the West Indies! Once the ear is attuned, all the dialects of Scots are immediately accessible, and if broadcast regularly would become as familiar as Oxford English.

One of the stock teachers' responses or excuses for not allowing the use of Scots in class is that their duty is to teach Standard English and that to encourage the dialects would be to sow seeds of confusion in the children. Nonsense! This is part of the monolingual world picture refuted by the experience of multilingual communities such as Switzerland. It is the attempt to eradicate the children's home language that has created the confusion. But the belief that there is only one acceptable speech form is so all-pervasive, so engrained and all-consuming, the counter-argument so rarely voiced that an alternative bilingual policy is literally unimaginable, even among people who are themselves bilingual.

Yet an active bilingual policy where both Scots and English are fostered and encouraged is surely the only logical way forward. Scots will not go away, the death-wish curse that has been upon it since the 18th century has gone unfulfilled. For the raucle tongue is a thrawn craitur that will bide on an on, tholan ilka dint fowk hes thrown at it. Even Scots who were not raised to speak it are affected by it and frequently fascinated by it. The publishing success of both Lorimer's translation of the *New Testament in Scots* and the *Concise Scots Dictionary*, and the massive public response to 'The Mother Tongue' and the 'Scots Tongue' television and radio series prove that people care about Scots. They will continue to care about it.

There should be no tension between English and Scots; they are branches of the same tree and are mutually intelligible and complementary to one another. Yet they are keys to radically different world pictures. I am delighted that I am a native speaker of a national variety of English, the most powerful, prestigious and useful language in the world. But as English has become the world's lingua franca, it has become rootless and impersonal. For some Scots, it has always been that. But its role as the medium of international dialogue has made it more alien as it has been twisted to conceal, rather than tell the truth. For the Pentagon during the Vietnam war, the term de-escalation often meant bombing densely-populated areas and napalming children. Nearer home, to the present Government and their allies, the captains of industry, the word rationalisation is used as a smokescreen behind which they hide as their victims are condemned to the misery of long-term unemployment.

In contrast, the power of Scots is its lack of duplicity, its vigorous directness, its ability to see through the false and the phony – the language reflecting the perspective of the kind of people who have been using it for the past century. William MacIlvanney put it well in the interview I did with him for 'The Mother Tongue':

> 'There is a value in Scots that you don't get in English. . . in the language itself, and what I would hope is that value is transferred to the way you think. To put it very simply, I think Scots is like English in it's underwear, you know it likes to dismantle pretensions..to the underwear. You know you can't fake it, you can't be as hypocritical, I think it's very difficult to be pompous in Scots. . . what I would hope is that the long tradition of language that we have, whatever happens to it in the future, would have engrained in us as a habit of thought, that kind of attitude.

Because language itself helps form the thoughts we have about our environment, Scots has a unique role as the tongue which is rooted deeply in the physical landscape we inhabit and has expressed our relationship with it for hundreds of years. If Scots were to disappear we would lose part of our sensitivity to our environment, because no other language can describe it with the same "feel"; a snell founeran wind that wad gar yer banes chitter, a dreich haar happin aa thing alang the coast, a douce simmer's gloamimg that's saft an bonnie, a thrang city street wi fowk breengin aboot an joukin atween ane anither.

It is also the language that describes perfectly the human types that inhabit this landscape; a sleekit big scunner. . . a braw, sonsie lassie. . . a gleg wean. . . a sapsie muckle-hertit sumph. . . .a thrawn besom. . . a shuilpit wee nyaff. . . a bachle wi no eneuch sough tae sprachle oot a sheugh. . . a kenspeckle honest guidman. . . in fact, the haill jingbang o sister an "brither Scots frae Maidenkirk tae John O' Groats." Scots is as essential to Scotland as her folk, her towns, her fields and rivers. It is part of Scotland. That is why it endures. I disagree with MacDiarmid's pessimistic view of the present, but I am sure he gets it right when he refers to past and future.

> For we hae faith in Scotland's hidden poo'ers
> The present's theirs, but a' the past and future's oors.

# Further Reading and Bibliography

Aitken, A.J. ed *The Dictionary of the Older Scottish Tongue* Aberdeen University Press.

Aitken, A.J. *Lowland Scots* Association for Scottish Literary Studies, Occasional Papers No 2, Edinburgh 1973.

Aitken, A.J. and McArthur, Tom. eds. *Languages of Scotland* W & R Chambers, Edinburgh 1979.

Akenson, D.H. and Crawford, W.H. *Local Poets and Social History: James Orr, Bard of Ballycarry.* Public Record Office of Northern Ireland, 1977.

Buchan, N and Hall, P. eds. *The Scottish Folksinger* Collins, Glasgow and London, 1973.

Burton, J.H. ed. *The Autobiography of Dr. Alexander Carlyle of Inveresk.* Foulis, Edinburgh 1910.

Connolly, Linde *Spoken English in Ulster in the 18th and 19th Centuries.* Ulster Folk Life, Vol 28, 1982.

Daiches, David *Literature and Gentility in Scotland* Edinburgh University Press, Edinburgh 1982.

Daiches, David, ed. *A Companion to Scottish Culture* Edward Arnold, London 1981.

Davie, George Elder *The Democratic Intellect* Edinburgh University Press 1961.

Elliott, Charles, ed. *Robert Henryson Poems* O.U.P. 1963.

Gibbon, Lewis Grassic *A Scots Quair* Hutchinson, London 1946.

Görlach, Manfred, ed. *Focus On: Scotland* John Benjamins Publishing Company, Amsterdam and Philadelphia 1985.

Glauser, Beat *The Scottish-English Linguistic Border* Francke Verlag Bern 1974

Graham, H.G. *Scottish Men of Letters in the Eighteenth Century* London 1901.

Graham, John J. *The Shetland Dictionary* Shetland Publishing Company, Lerwick, 1984

Graham, William *The Scots Word Book* Ramsay Head Press, Edinburgh 1977.

Grant, W. and Dixon, J.M. eds. *Manual of Modern Scots* Cambridge 1921.

Grieve, Michael, and Scott, Alexander, eds. *The Hugh MacDiarmid Anthology* Routledge and Kegan Paul, London 1972.

Haugen, E., McClure, J.D., Thomson, D.S. eds. *Minority Languages Today* Edinburgh University Press, Edinburgh 1981.

Jack, R.D.S. ed. *Scottish Prose 1550–1700* Calder & Boyars London 1971.

Jones, Richard Foster *The Triumph of the English Language* O.U.P. 1953.

Kratzmann, Gregory *Anglo-Scottish Literary Relations 1430–1530* Cambridge University Press 1980

Leonard, Tom *Intimate Voices: Selected Works 1965–1983* Galloping Dog Press Glasgow 1984.

Macafee, Caroline *Glasgow* (Varieties of English Around the World) Benjamins Amsterdam 1983.

Mackenzie, W. Mackay, ed. *The Poems of William Dunbar* Faber and Faber London 1932.

MacQueen, J. and Scott, T. eds. *The Oxford Book of Scottish Verse O.U.P. 1965*.

McClure, J.D. ed. *Scotland and the Lowland Tongue* Aberdeen University Press, 1983.

McClure, J.D., Aitken, A.J., Low, J.T. eds. *The Scots Language. Planning for Modern Usage* Ramsay Head Press, Edinburgh 1980.

McDiarmid, M.P. ed. *The Poems of Robert Fergusson* Scottish Text Society Edinburgh 1954.

McIlvanney, William *Docherty* Mainstream Publishing, Edinburgh 1983.

McNeill, P, and Nicholson, R., eds. *An Historical Atlas of Scotland* c.400–c.1600. St Andrews 1975.

Mather, James Y and Speitel, H.H., eds. *The Linguistic Atlas of Scotland*, Scots Section vols 1 & 2. Croom Helm, London 1975/1977.

Millar, J.H. *A Literary History of Scotland* London 1903.

Murison, David. *The Guid Scots Tongue* Blackwood, Edinburgh 1977.

Murison, David, ed. *The Scottish National Dictionary*

Nicolaisen, W.F.H. *Scottish Place Names* B.T. Batsford, London 1976.

Price, Glanville. *The Languages of Britain* Edward Arnold, 1984

Robinson, Mairi, ed. *The Concise Scots Dictionary* Aberdeen University Press Aberdeen, 1985.

Royle, Trevor. *The Macmillan Companion to Scottish Literature* Macmillan, London 1983.

Scott, P.H. *In Bed With an Elephant: The Scottish Experience* Saltire Pamphlets, The Saltire Society, Edinburgh 1984.

Shreeves, W.P. *A Study in the Language of Scottish Prose Before 1600*. John Murphy & Co. Baltimore 1893.

Smith, G Gregory *Specimens of Middle Scots* Blackwood, Edinburgh 1902.

Stephens, Meic *Linguistic Minorities in Western Europe* Gomer Press, Llandysul 1976.

Trudgill, Peter, ed. *Language in the British Isles* Cambridge University Press 1984.

Ulster Folk Museum. *Ulster Dialects. An Introductory Symposium.* Hollywood Co. Down 1964.

Watson, Roderick. *The Literature of Scotland* Macmillan, London 1984.

Williams, Gordon *From Scenes Like These* London 1968.

Williamson, A.H. *Scottish National Consciousness in the Age of James VI* John Donald, Edinburgh 1979

Wilson, Sir J. *The Dialects of Central Scotland* Oxford 1926.

Wolfe J.N. ed. *Government and Nationalism in Scotland* E.U.P., Edinburgh 1969.

*Periodicals:*

*Lallans* William Neill ed. The Scots Language Society. (quarterly)

*Scottish Language* H.H.Speitel ed., Association for Scottish Literary Studies. (annually)

Members of both organisations receive the journals free of charge.

*Addresses:*

David Dyer
Thesaurer, Scots Language Society
4 Seafield Court
Aberdeen AB1 7IY

Dr David Hewitt
Treasurer, Association for Scottish Literary Studies
Department of English
University of Aberdeen
Aberdeen AB9 2UB

Scottish National Dictionary Association
27, George Square
Edinburgh EH8

Cassette recordings across the whole range of Scots are available from
Scotsoun
13 Ashton Rd
Glasgow G12 8SP

The author has recorded an L.P. of the poetry of Robert Fergusson and the traditional music of his day. 'Fergusson's Auld Reekie' is on Iona Records. Music is by Rod Paterson, Derek Hoy, Tony Cuffe and Norman Chalmers.

# Index

Aberdeen 163
Addison, Joseph 91
Aitken, A J 138
Alexander II 31
Alexander III 36
Alexander, William 164
Alexander, William, Earl of Stirling 76
Anderson, Basil 167
Andrew of Wyntoun 36
Annand, J K 137, 163
Arbroath, Declaration of 37-8
Arbuthnott, Dr 100
Ariosto, Ludovico 48
Auchinleck, Lord 83
Auld Alliance 33, 71
Avoch 164
Ayton, Robert 72
Bacon, Francis 75, 80
Bann, River 155
Bannatyne Club 112
Bannatyne Miscellany 56
Bannockburn, battle of 36
Barbour, John 36
Beaton, Cardinal 66
Beattie, James 91, 93, 107
Bellenden, John 55
Ben Yehuda *see* Perlmann, Eliezer
Berwick 159
Blacklock, Thomas 93
Blin Hary 38, 96
Boece, Hector 55
Border ballads 104
Boswell, James 82-5, 89, 107
Bowhill 15, 152
Boyd, Mark Alexander 69-70
Boyd, Zachary 72
Braxfield, Lord 108, 123
Brown, George Douglas 116, 118
Bruce, Robert the 36-7
Buchanan, George 48, 69, 95
Buchanan, James 86
Bulter, Rhoda 167

Burghead 161
Burns, Robert 15, 17, 38, 41, 77, 93, 96-7, 100-105, 109, 117, 130-1, 146, 156-7, 164
Byron 170
Campbell, Donald 137
Campbell, Thomas 107
Carham 29
Carlyle, Alexander 91-2
Castalian Band 69-72
Caxton, William 51-2
Chartier, Alain 54
Chaucer, Geoffrey 48, 49, 51, 53, 65, 175
Chepman and Myllar 46
Clatt 162-3
Clerk of Penicuik, John 108
Cockburn, Lord 75, 111-2, 123, 153
Coldstream 22, 24, 72
Complaynt of Scotland, The 53, 58
*Concise Scots Dictionary* 177
Congalton, Dr Charles 92
Constable, Henry 69
Cornhill 22, 24, 72
Country Life Archive 138
Craigmillar Castle 47
Crawfurd, Andrew 122
Crockett, Evelyn 133
Crockett, S R 117
Cruikshank, Helen B 152
Cullen, Walter 149
Cumnock 172
Cunningsburgh 166
Daiches, David 71, 172
Dalrymple, Father James 55
Darvel 151
David I 31-32
*Dictionary of the Older Scottish Tongue* 137
Donaldson, William 119
Douglas, Gavin 39, 41-2, 49, 52-3, 95, 155
Douglas, James 35
Drummond of Hawthornden, William 77
Du Bartas, Guillaume de Salluste 69
Du Bellay, Joachim 69
Dunbar, William 41, 43-9, 53, 69, 152
Duncan, J B 120
Duncan, King 29
Dundee 150-2

Dunfermline 152
Edgar, King 31
Edinburgh 125, 133, 152-3
Edward I of England 37-8
Edward the Confessor 31
Elliot, Walter 159
Elphinstone, James 90
Erskine of Dun, Miss 113
Esquierdo, Mr 172
Fergusson, Robert 77, 93, 96-8, 105, 156
Ferrier, Susan 116
Flodden, battle of 46
Fort William 151
Fowler, William 72
Francis I of France 140
François III of France 47
Galston 15, 151
Galt, John 116
Garioch, Robert 131
Garry, Flora 162
Gau, John 64-5
Germersheim 176
Gibbon, Lewis Grassic 27, 62, 162, 170-1
Glasgow 121, 150-1, 153-4, 164, 171-3, 177
Glauser, Beat 23
Godskirk and Hume 86
Görlach, Manfred, 146
Gower, John 50
Graham, Helen 169
Graham, Reverend John 155
Graham, John G 166
Greig, Gavin 120
Grey, Thomas 160
Grieve, Christopher Murray *see* Hugh MacDiarmid
Guthrie, Will 65
Hamilton, William 60
Hamilton of Bangour, William 95
Hamilton of Gilbertfield, William 95-6
Hardie, Keir 175
Hay, Sir Gilbert 55
Henderson, Hamish 78, 136
Henry IV of England 35
Henry VIII of England 61
Henryson, Robert 41-3, 46, 53
Herder, J G 171
Hill Burton, John 114

Hogg, James 109, 116
Holinshed, Raphael 55
Hopeman 161
Hume, Alexander 69, 80-1
Hume, David 85, 88, 90-2, 102
Hume of Polwart, Patrick 69
Hutton, James 92
Ireland, John of 55
Irvine Valley 63, 154
Jacob, Violet 113, 152
Jakobsen, Jakob 166
James I 53, 65
James II 35
James IV 39, 46, 52, 69, 152
James V 45, 47, 52, 60, 71
James VI, 68-9, 70-1, 75, 80, 149, 155
Jamieson, John 112
Jeffrey, Francis 111, 123-4
John o'Groats 165
Johnson, Samuel 82-4
Jonson, Ben 77
Kailyard 116-8, 130
Kay, Billy 134, 171
Kelman, James 135
Kelvinside 123-4
Kemp, Robert 134
Kennedy, Walter 69
Kennedy Erskine of Dun, Miss *see* Jacob, Violet
Kerr, J 113
Kilmarnock 17
King, Inspector 115
Knox, John 57, 59-60, 66-7
Kyle 15, 103, 118
Langholm 130
Lauder, Harry 125
Lekpreuik, Robert 63
Leonard, Tom 135
Lerwick 151
Leslie, Bishop 47, 55
Lindesay of Pitscottie, Robert 55, 67
Linguistic Survey of Scotland 137
Linlithgow 152
Little France 47
Lochhead, Liz 134
Lochwinnoch 121
Lockhart, J G 111-2, 123

Logan 172
Lorimer, W L 152, 177
Lossiemouth 133, 161
Lydgate, John 65
Lyndsay, Sir David 20, 41, 44-5, 47, 61, 130, 134
MacAlpin, Kenneth 28
MacColla, Fionn 174
MacDiarmid, Hugh 19, 41, 96, 119, 130-3, 140, 179
MacKenzie of Rosehaugh, Sir George 81
MacKenzie, Henry 93, 108-9
Maclaren, Ian 117-8
Madeleine de Valois 47, 71
Maitland Club 112
Malcolm II 29
Malcolm III or Canmore 31
Mansfield, Lord 92
Margaret, Queen 31
Marie de Guise 47, 57
Marwick, Hugh 166
Mary, Queen of Scots 47, 65, 67
Masson, Mr 89
Mauchline 15
McAllister, Alex 157
McClure, J Derrick 105-7, 138, 146, 173
McIlroy, Archibald 157
McIlvanney, William 17, 102, 127, 129, 178
McLellan, Robert 87, 134, 136-7
Melville, James 67
Melvin, Mr 114
Millar, A H 124
Milne, J C 162
Mistral, Frederic 140
Montgomerie, Alexander 34, 69-71
Morer, Reverend Thomas 78
Morningside 123
Muir, Mr 115
Murray, Charles 118, 162
Murray, John 18
Myll, Maister 56
Napoleon 140
Neill, William 137
Newmilns 63
Nicol, William 101
Nicoll, John 76
Nisbet, Murdoch 63-4
Noble, William 88

Northumbria, Earl of 29
Nudrye, William 66
Oftedal, Magde 148
Oliphant, Mrs 116
Orr, James 156-7
Owein of Strathclyde 29
Pedersen, Christiern 64
Pedro de Ayala 39, 65
Perlmann, Eliezer 145
Perry, William 89-90
Perth 152
Perth, Lady 113
Pinkerton, John 105
Pope, Alexander 91, 94, 100
Porter, Hugh 156
Purves, David 138
Puttenham, George 50
Ramsay, Allan 77, 93-6, 98-100, 105
Ramsay, Allan (painter) 85
Ramsay, Dean 112-3
Robert of Gloucester 50
Robertson, Jeannie 136
Robertson, William 92
Robinson, Mairi 62
Ronsard, Pierre de 71
Rorie, David 162
Ross, Alexander 107, 162
Ruddiman, Thomas 95
Ruthwell, Kirk of 29
Saltire Society 138
School of Scottish Studies 138
Scots Confession, The 62-3
Scott, Alexander 131, 137
Scott, Sir Walter 92, 109, 111-2, 116-7, 133, 146, 176
Scott, William 86
Scottish Chaucerians 48
Scottish National Dictionary 137, 151, 158, 165, 172
Sempill of Beltrees, Robert 77
Shakespeare, William 55
Shenstone, William 91
Sheridan, Thomas 89, 107
Shetland Dictionary 150, 167
Simpson, Habbie 77
Skelton, John 53
Skene, Sir John 63
Smith, Adam 91

Smith, Sidney Goodsir 131, 134
Soutar, William 131, 152
Spencer, Edward 175
St Andrews 64
Standard Habbie 77
Stevenson, R L 116-9
Stewart of Baldynneis, John 69
Stuart, Esmé, Seigneur d'Aubigny 71
Surrey, Henry Howard, earl of 53
Thomson, James 107
Tyndale, William 62
Villon, François 48
Virgil 52
Wallace, William 37-8
Wars of Independence 36
Watson, James 95
Wedderburne, Alexander 107
Williams, Gordon 126
Williams, William Carlos 135
Williamson, Keith 76
Wycliffe, John 64
Wynyet, Ninian 60
Yetholm 159
Young, Douglas 131